GS Misc 401

THEOLOGICAL T

A WAY AHEAD

A Report to the House of Bishops of the General Synod of the Church of England

by

The Steering Group for Theological Courses

and

The Advisory Group on Full-Time Theological Training

October 1992

CHURCH HOUSE PUBLISHING
Church House, Great Smith Street, London SW1P 3NZ

ISBN 0 7151 3748 4
GS Misc 401
Published 1992 for the General Synod of the Church of England
by Church House Publishing

Printed in England by Rapier Press Ltd

PREFACE

Most people will, I think, acknowledge the difficulties which the two Groups have faced in producing this Report. The Theological Colleges and Courses of the Church of England are independent institutions and almost wholly autonomous. The Church of England itself is struggling to come to terms with the issue of the Ordination of Women to the Priesthood. The national scene in Higher Education is changing rapidly and dramatically. Economic pressures show little sign of abating and, alongside questions of vocation and recruitment for professional ministry, lie issues of Stewardship and of what we should afford as an institutional Church.

Nevertheless, our work on this Report has given much to encourage and cheer us. It is our firm belief that theological teachers in our Church are of good professional standing. Students are better taught than in the past and go to considerable lengths to fulfil what is asked of them in their training.

The overriding concern of both Groups has been the need of the Church of England for training and ministerial formation which is theologically appropriate, educationally effective, adequately resourced and affordable. The recent decline in numbers of ordination candidates and the financial effects of this have given urgency to our review of the existing Colleges and Courses. In considering the needs of the future, we have taken the firm view that change must be managed and not simply left to market forces, as these could have unforeseen and undesirable effects. Short term decisions should be consonant with the Church's longer term needs. Fortunately, as a result of work undertaken by the College and Course staffs, in response to ACCM Paper No. 22, there is now much more clarity as to the training needed for the kind of ministry which the Church requires.

This report concludes one process and initiates another. We have analysed the problems facing theological education and make recommendations to the House of Bishops which, if adopted, will lead to change for all the Colleges and Courses. We emphasise the need for progress in the implementation of these changes to be monitored effectively. This will help ensure that the best use is made of resources and that the General Synod receives value for money.

We have taken careful account of the different traditions within the Church, reflected in both the Colleges and the Courses, and have sought to be even-handed in our conclusions. We have tried to respect the independence of the institutions and the freedom of choice of candidates. To be more firm would have required central direction of ordination candidates to particular institutions and we did not consider that this was either desirable or necessary at the present time.

Both our Groups have enjoyed whole-hearted co-operation from representatives of the Methodist and United Reformed Churches; both John Taylor and Michael Dunford have often helped us see the Church of England's predicament in a wider perspective and pointed the way towards future co-operation. Given the changes in the Higher Education scene, there is scope for us to relate in new ways to other educational institutions and, in particular, we have received generous help on these matters from Sinclair Goodlad, who has represented the Council of Church and Associated Colleges. We have been marvellously served by our Secretary, John Newton. His award of a well-deserved Lambeth MA gave particular pleasure to the members of both Groups. The Groups have worked together with skill, happiness and dedication and have been greatly assisted by the educational knowledge and experience of Brian Russell of the ABM staff.

We offer this Report to the House of Bishops to assist them in discussing a way ahead for theological education.

It has been a privilege for me to act as the Chairman of the two Groups.

30.9.92 + ROBERT LINCOLN:

TABLE OF CONTENTS

ABBREVIATIONS

ABM	Advisory Board of Ministry
ACCM	Advisory Council for the Church's Ministry
ACCM 22	ACCM Occasional Paper No.22: *Education for the Church's Ministry*
ACCM 30	ACCM Occasional Paper No.30: *Report of the Working Party on the Structure and Financing of Theological Courses*
ACOCF	The Anglo-Catholic Ordination Candidates Fund
AOCM	Association of Ordinands and Candidates for Ministry
CATS	Credit Accumulation and Transfer
CBF	Central Board of Finance
CCAC	Council of Church and Associated Colleges
CCHE	Church College of Higher Education
CDTI	Carlisle Diocesan Training Institute
CME	Continuing Ministerial Education
CNAA	Council for National Academic Awards
CSM	Canterbury School of Ministry
CTE	Committee for Theological Education
EAMTC	East Anglian Ministerial Training Course
EMMTC	East Midlands Ministry Training Course
EVSC	Educational Validation Sub-Committee (of IMEC)

GSM	Gloucester School for Ministry
IMEC	Initial Ministerial Education Committee (of the ABM)
LEA	Local Education Authority
LNSM	Local Non-Stipendiary Ministry
NEOC	North East Ordination Course
NOC	Northern Ordination Course
OHMTC	Oak Hill Ministerial Training Course
OMC	Oxford Ministry Course
POT	Post Ordination Training
RSC	Recruitment and Selection Committee (of the ABM)
SADMTS	St Albans Diocese Ministerial Training Scheme
SDMTS	Southern Dioceses Ministerial Training Scheme
SOC	Southwark Ordination Course

SWMTC	South West Ministerial Training Course
URC	United Reformed Church
WMMTC	West Midlands Ministerial Training Course
WSIHE	West Sussex Institute of Higher Education

THEOLOGICAL TRAINING: A WAY AHEAD

A. INTRODUCTION

1. This Report is about the need of the Church of England for training and ministerial formation which is theologically appropriate, educationally effective, adequately resourced and affordable. It describes the work of two Groups which have been reviewing the Theological Colleges and Courses and considering other provision made for ministerial training. It comes at a time when theological training is under pressure both from changes in educational practice and from the financial problems caused by reduced numbers of students. Because the nature of the tasks given by the House of Bishops to the two Groups differed, it is necessary to describe their work in separate sections of this Report. Nevertheless, we wish to emphasise that the Groups have had a common Chairman, common members from the Methodist and United Reformed Churches and common staffing; the Groups have liaised closely during their work and met jointly on several occasions to formulate this Report.

2. As will be seen, the proposals put forward by the two Groups for urgent action in the short term are compatible with, and lead on to, an overall long-term strategy for the theological training of ordinands in the Church of England. The long-term strategy has regard to the needs of the Dioceses for lay training and for the in-service training of the clergy and to the ordination training requirements of the Methodist and United Reformed Churches. The Roman Catholic and Baptist Churches and the Centre for Black and White Christian Partnership have also been consulted.

3. Each Group has had available to it evidence from the institutions under review and from the relevant committees of the Advisory Board of Ministry.* It has analysed the problems and possibilities in its own area of reference and takes responsibility for the recommendations relating to these. The Groups, however, take joint responsibility for the coherence of their recommendations and for the proposals

* *The Advisory Board of Ministry (ABM) succeeded the Advisory Council for the Church's Ministry (ACCM) on 1st April, 1991.*

made in this report for a strategy for the way ahead. (The use of "we" in this Report thus relates to both Groups, except in section C when it refers to the Steering Group and in section D to the Advisory Group.)

B. THEOLOGICAL TRAINING IN THE CHURCH OF ENGLAND

4. The Church of England formally recognises 14 independent Theological Colleges and the same number of part-time Theological Courses in England as institutions for the training of ordinands and accredited lay workers sponsored by English Bishops. Such candidates may also train at Coates Hall, Edinburgh and St Michael's College, Llandaff. A description of the training offered at each of these institutions is given in Advisory Board of Ministry's publication: *Theological Training in the Church of England**. A copy of the relevant parts of this is included as an Addendum to this report. The publication also gives the text of the relevant Bishops' Regulations (pp.81-91) and of pre-theological training courses (pp.95-6). In addition, it is possible for mature candidates to receive ordination training, tailored to their individual needs, at St Deiniol's Library, Hawarden, subject to authorisation by the Recruitment and Selection Committee (RSC) of ABM.

5. In the last five years there have been fundamental changes in training for ordained ministry in the Church of England. These have taken place largely as a result of the implementation of ACCM Occasional Paper No.22, *Education for the Church's Ministry* (ACCM 22). A paper prepared by ABM's Initial Ministerial Education Committee (IMEC) is attached as Appendix A to this report. It describes in detail these educational developments. As shown in Part III.B of the Appendix (see page 129), each Theological College and Course seeking formal recognition through validation of its syllabus and curriculum by the Educational Validation Sub-Committee (EVSC) of IMEC is required to state what it sees as the theological basis for ministerial training. It is asked to relate this to God's presence and action in the world and in the Church, as Creator and Saviour; to give attention to the Church's mission as well as its ministry; and

* *The material on each College or Course is provided by the institution itself.*

to explore the relation between ordained ministry and lay ministry. These responses are expected to lead to a clear set of objectives for training and to include a rationale and a clear plan for the educational programme. They must also provide a plan for assessment to gauge whether individual students have met the training objectives.

6. IMEC's paper sets the overall scene by explaining that, whereas students in the Colleges train largely on the basis of three academic terms a year plus a period of 4 to 6 weeks in placements, those on the Courses train largely through weekly tutorial groups, backed up by between 8 and 10 hours of private study each week, together with from 5 to 9 residential weekends each year and an annual summer school.

7. It offers the following profile of students* sponsored by English Bishops and training in 1991:

i) **Age:** Stipendiary men - nearly 50% aged 30 or over.
Stipendiary women - over 70% aged 30 or over.
NSMs - normally all aged over 30.
Increasing trend towards older candidates amongst women.

ii) Colleges: 16% women: 84% men.
55% are married ordinands.
254 of the candidates under 30 were reading for a theology degree.

iii) Courses: 55% women: 45% men.
Proportion of stipendiary candidates training on Courses rather than full-time in Colleges is higher for women than for men.

IMEC concludes from this profile that increasing attention has had to

* *The total number of sponsored Church of England ordinands in Theological Colleges was about 1,400 in the early 1960's and about 760 in the early 1990's. The Courses only began to exist during the 1960's. In the early 1990's they had about 370 sponsored Church of England ordinands.*

be given to teaching, finance and accommodation for older men and women, often with family responsibilities.

8. The paper describes how, following the decline in the use of the General Ministerial Examination, it was necessary to re-establish a common basis for theological training. This has been achieved through the procedure of validation and assessment laid down in ACCM 22. Over the last 5 years, all the Colleges and Courses have submitted details of their theological basis, educational programmes and plans for student assessment to the EVSC. Such validation has to be confirmed every 5 years. The validation is backed up by a cadre of External Examiners, who monitor the effectiveness of the educational programmes, and by the Bishops' Inspectors, who assess the institutions for their theological training and their preparation of students for ordination.

9. Reviewing the first 5 years of the process, IMEC has observed increased emphasis on mission, communication skills and preparation for collaborative ministry; a clearer theological basis for training; better coordination of the various elements in training; more purposeful staff development and more appreciation of the need to link initial training to post-ordination training (POT) and continuing ministerial education (CME). Analysis of these developments has been fed back to the Colleges and Courses in two reports: ABM Ministry Papers Nos. 1 and 3*. IMEC concludes that this restructuring of theological education has been theologically based and practically oriented and that, whilst greater responsibility has been devolved to Colleges and Courses, proper accountability remains to the House of Bishops through the work of the ABM and the Bishops' Inspectors.

10. It is against this background of a more mature but decreasing student body and a re-modelled structure for theological education that the two Groups have approached their tasks. A broader discussion of educational issues affecting the future shape of theological training is to be found later in this Report (see paragraphs 91 to 125). First we describe the way in which the two Groups came into being and how they have approached their tasks.

* *Ordination and the Church's Ministry: ABM Ministry Paper No.1 and Integration and Assessment: ABM Ministry Paper No.3*

C. PART-TIME THEOLOGICAL COURSES

a) Formation of the Steering Group

11. A Working Party on the Structure and Finance of Theological Courses, chaired by the Bishop of Tewkesbury, reported to the House of Bishops in January 1989. Its Report was published as ACCM Occasional Paper No.30 (ACCM 30) and sent for consultation to Course Principals and their Governing Bodies. The recommendations of ACCM 30 are re-printed as Appendix B to this Report.

12. The responses from the Courses stressed the serious financial position of a number of Courses and the need for decisions to be taken urgently. There was unanimous support for the idea of block grants but certain elements of the proposed educational criteria attracted criticism.

13. The Working Party had found that educational and financial considerations were, in fact, inter-related. A course that met the size criterion for educational viability would also be likely to be financially viable. Conversely, too much deviation from the educational factors would not only be educationally undesirable but would also remove the basis for financial viability. In putting forward the responses to the House of Bishops, ACCM Council commented that the central Church could only be expected to make the block grants required to ensure a stable network of non-residential Courses provided that these were large enough to justify the cost and to meet the Church's needs for ordination training. It pointed out that the Working Party had not recommended one particular educational model nor sought to impose a pre-determined geographical pattern of organisation. Rather, it had set out the basic factors which it believed to be necessary for any part-time course of ordination training and had proposed that a Steering Group should discuss the details in each locality. This was intended to provide flexibility and the opportunity for consideration to be paid to specific local needs.

14. On 19th June 1989, the House of Bishops endorsed the recommendations of the Report* and resolved that Courses should only be recognised for ordination training if:

i) their syllabus and curriculum had been validated by ACCM's Courses and Examinations Sub-Committee (now the Educational Validation Sub-Committee of ABM) under the assessment procedures set out in ACCM 22;

ii) ACCM had certified that the proposals for each Course represented an adequate response to the minimum requirements recommended in the Report (ACCM 30) with regard to educational factors, staffing levels and management structure.

The House also agreed that negotiation and agreement of the arrangements should be concluded by 31st August 1992 and that all the new arrangements should be implemented before the end of a further two-year period.

15. The House decided that a Steering Group should be set up to assist groups of dioceses to establish new organisations which met the requirements of the Report.

16. The Steering Group for Theological Courses was accordingly established in October 1989 with the following terms of reference and membership:

Terms of Reference

i) To convene meetings of interested parties with a view to securing the implementation of the recommendations of the Working Party.

ii) To advise on the educational, financial and constitutional arrangements for the new organisations in the light of the recommendations in the Report.

* *Except Recommendation 51: see footnote in Appendix B.*

iii) To act as a catalyst in the transitional arrangements.

iv) To help resolve any associated financial problems.

v) To report annually to the House of Bishops on progress with implementation.

Membership

The Rt Revd Robert Hardy, Bishop of Lincoln (Chairman);

The Ven Jonathan Bailey, Archdeacon of Southend and Bishop-designate of Dunwich;

The Revd Canon Ronald Coppin, Canon Residentiary of Durham and Chairman of the Inspections Working Party;

Miss Janet Trotter, OBE, Director of Cheltenham and Gloucester College of Higher Education and Bishops' Inspector of Theological Colleges and Courses (formerly, member of ACCM 30 Working Party);

*The Revd John Taylor (General Secretary, Division of Ministries, Methodist Church);

*The Revd Michael Dunford (until June 1992 Secretary for Ministerial Training, United Reformed Church).

Staff: Mr John Newton - Secretary (formerly Administrative Secretary, ACCM/ABM)
The Revd Dr Brian Russell (Secretary to IMEC)

* *The representatives from the Methodist and United Reformed Churches were originally invited to be consultants to the Group; in fact they have acted as full members from the beginning.*

b) **Initial Consultation**

17. At the outset, the Steering Group heard detailed accounts given by the representatives of each diocese as to its ministerial training needs, both in terms of existing diocesan policy and future aspirations. The Group then engaged in a series of meetings with representatives from the existing part-time Courses to discuss how far they met the educational, financial and constitutional criteria endorsed by the House, and the needs expressed by individual dioceses.

c) **A Regional Structure for Courses**

18. From the beginning of its discussions, the Steering Group had been concerned at the fragility of many of the Courses. Student numbers over the past ten years (see Appendix C) illustrate the small cadre of Church of England ordinands likely to be present in each year-group of these three-year Courses. Even with the participation, in some cases, of Methodist and United Reformed Church candidates, the numbers of ordination candidates have often been significantly below those envisaged in ACCM 30 as the minimum educationally viable (see Appendix B, recommendation 9).

19. The small Courses usually have only 1, 1.5 or 2 members of core teaching staff, which may mean they have to work a good deal in isolation. This level of core staff poses problems for covering all the activities of the Course and for giving effective pastoral care to dispersed students. The pattern of staffing places great strain on one or two individuals, but may incidentally offer an illustration of effective teamwork. The core staff will often have to work with experts in various disciplines brought in individually to teach on and help with the Course; the staff may also have to hold together a number of widely scattered tutors. These tasks require particular managerial skills, however, which may not be reflected in the core staff. The pressure of keeping a Course running throughout the year makes it difficult for a small core staff to find time for revision of the syllabus and curriculum or opportunities for staff development within a peer group. Similarly an impending Inspection can become a major logistical problem.

20. For all these reasons and despite the fact that ACCM 30 accepted 1.5 as a minimum staff size, the Steering Group reached the conclusion

that ideally each part-time Course needed to be resourced across a Region large enough to warrant a core teaching staff of four or five. This staff group would cover a range of specialisms and have the resilience to be creative educationally, to draw on the other resources of theological education available in the Region and, in turn, to contribute to meeting the needs of the Dioceses and other Churches locally for lay and in-service training.

21. The Steering Group has therefore encouraged groupings of Courses to set up a Forum in their Region to facilitate conversations with other theological training resources in the Region (eg. University Departments, Colleges of Higher Education, Theological Colleges across denominations) and with representatives of dioceses and of the other Churches. The aim was to determine the most appropriate structure for part-time ordination training in that area, and the extent to which it should be associated with training for other types of ministry.

d) Policy and Guidelines

22. During the initial process of consultation, the Steering Group clarified its own thinking as to what were the essential considerations if the aims of ACCM 30 were to be achieved. These can be summarised as follows:

1) A national network of Courses, able to deliver, both for the Church of England and for the other Churches, high quality ordination training on a part-time basis. Such a network should reflect regional identities and could build on the contribution and expertise of the existing Courses.

2) This national network should be acceptable throughout to the Methodist and United Reformed Churches so that use of the structure can be on an ecumenical basis in every part of the country.

3) Each Course within the national network should be able to respond to the needs and prior learning of individuals and to provide training through suitably varied teaching methods and structures (eg. teaching centres, local tutors,

written study units). This should reflect the best practice of current adult educational methods.

4) Each Course should be open to the possibility of selling its expertise by offering other training in response to local needs (eg. LNSM training, Reader training, other lay training and adult education) so as to maximise the use of finite human and financial resources.

5) Affirmation of the priorities established by the ACCM 22 procedure (see Appendix A) ie. that initial training should be:

   i) carried out in a way that is inter-disciplinary and with scope for the integration of theology and practice;

   ii) part of a continuing process of ministerial formation and development;

   iii) carried out in a way that enshrines collaborative values with regard, for example, to the style of training and to the mode of operation of the Course;

   iv) an appropriate preparation for ordained ministers to serve the mission of God in the light of the world-wide ecumenical context.

6) The desirability of the new arrangements being disposable in form so that future generations are not faced with a 1990's approach fixed in tablets of stone.

23. The Steering Group also reached the conclusion that, if a network was to be established nationally in line with these essential considerations, the structure for each new Regional Course would need to have the following characteristics:

i) The one Regional Course should be organised so that it is able to deliver, in appropriately varying ways, in all parts of the region.

ii) The control and management of all the activities of the Course within the Region should lie with a single Governing Body.

iii) The members of staff throughout the Region should constitute one staff team.

iv) One submission under the ACCM 22 procedure should cover all the ordination training activities of the Course.

v) The whole Course should be covered by common External Examiners acting for the sponsoring Churches.

vi) A single budget should be presented annually to the ABM Finance Committee, showing (a) the cost of all ordination training and (b) the cost of other activities carried out by the Course. These costs should be based on the fixed and variable costs guidelines set out in ACCM 30 (see Appendix B to this Report, recommendations 38-44). The ABM Finance Committee should be expected to consult with the other Churches in agreeing these budgets and the division between fixed and variable costs.

vii) All the ordination training activities of the Course should be embraced in a single quinquennial inspection on behalf of the sponsoring Churches.

e) **Method of Implementation**

24. To ensure that these essential considerations (see paragraph 22) and structural characteristics (see paragraph 23) were fully discussed in the conversations being held by the Courses in each Region, the Steering Group asked that the discussions in each "Regional Forum" should cover:

i) The philosophy of ministerial training and model of the Church's ministry.

ii) The educational model and approach to be adopted.

iii) Quality assurance.

iv) Structure of the proposed Regional Course.

v) Governing Body and Management.

vi) Resources available.

vii) Timetable for implementation.

25. The Steering Group also suggested that once these topics had been discussed and an overall vision and strategy agreed by the Regional Forum, it should then move on to establish two task groups:

i) *a shadow Course Council* considering detailed matters of structure, government and resources;

ii) *a shadow Board of Studies* considering detailed matters of education and training, including the preparation of a new response under the ACCM 22 procedure (a pre-requisite of formal recognition being granted by the sponsoring Churches - see paragraph 14.i) above).

f) Stage Reached

26. Because of variations in the size, philosophy and educational models of the fourteen existing part-time Theological Courses, it would not be realistic to expect them all to follow rigidly the same pattern of development. In setting out the Steering Group's views on the essential considerations and structural characteristics for future Regional Courses, we recognised that each part-time Course had its own individual characteristics and method of delivery and was constrained by the nature of the area of the country which it served. Discussions in the various Regions have therefore proceeded at different speeds and the Group has been anxious to allow sufficient flexibility to meet local circumstances. Nevertheless we are also clear that special pleading must not divert the Group from the task it was set of ensuring that "all ordination candidates living in England should have access to a high quality of training non-residentially for the ordained ministry" (ACCM 30, Recommendation 1). Against this

background, we now describe the stage reached in discussions in each Region by 1st September 1992.

27. ACCM 30 stressed that each Course must have an assured source of candidates from a defined geographical catchment area, but it noted that geographical factors did not always make it practicable for all the candidates from a Diocese to attend the same Course. It therefore envisaged groupings of Dioceses, each endorsing one or two local Courses.

28. The Steering Group accepts this general approach but wishes to add a gloss. It recognises that there are situations where the personal circumstances or educational needs of a particular candidate, or ease of travel, make it desirable for that person to train on an alternative Course. For instance, a long-distance commuter to London might be unable to attend a local teaching centre but find week-night attendance at the Southwark Ordination Course (SOC) centre in Blackfriars possible. Similarly, a shift worker might be unable to train unless linked to a Course with personal tutoring arrangements. To this extent, we believe that the Regional boundaries to which we refer below should be subject to some porosity.

29. It was clearly stated in ACCM 30 that the pattern of Courses suggested in paragraph 88 of that report was not intended as a master plan, but merely as an illustration of one way in which the principles recommended could be put into practice. The Steering Group has moved on from that position. After a great deal of discussion with local representatives throughout the country, it is now putting forward firm recommendations to the House of Bishops, in the paragraphs which follow, for a geographical pattern of part-time theological training in England based on eight Regions.

1) *The South East*

30. The South East Region covers the Dioceses of Southwark, Rochester and Canterbury. It is currently served by the Southwark Ordination Course and the Canterbury School of Ministry (CSM). Because of the location of its teaching centre at Blackfriars, SOC receives candidates from outside the Region who commute daily to work in London and also other candidates from the Dioceses of Chelmsford, Guildford and London. On the other hand, a number of candidates

from the Region attend the part-time Course at Oak Hill College in Southgate, mainly for churchmanship reasons. Both SOC and CSM train candidates from other Churches.

31. Following discussions between representatives of the two Courses, the Diocese of Rochester and the Steering Group, a task group was set up to report to the Governing Bodies of SOC and CSM as to the practicability of establishing a single Course to serve the whole Region. The aim was to create a free-standing, centrally administered Course with local outlets able to respond to the needs of the three Dioceses and of the Methodist and United Reformed Churches, primarily for ordination training. It is hoped that the new Regional Course will be capable of delivering also other types of ministerial training and education to meet local needs. The development of a third teaching centre, possibly in the Medway area is being considered.

32. Proposals for such a South East Theological Course* have recently been agreed by the three Dioceses and a Shadow Council and Board of Studies have been set up, including representatives of the other Churches. The Shadow Board of Studies is preparing a new response under the ACCM 22 procedure, setting out the educational programme for the new Regional Course. It will then consider the question of University validation. The previous link between SOC and the Extramural Department of London University is being severed; options for the future include the University of Kent at Canterbury, the University of Surrey through the Roehampton Institute and the University of London.

33. The membership of the Council of the new Course is expected to be agreed by the Shadow Council in September, 1992, after which work will proceed on details of the Constitution using the SOC model of a Charitable Company limited by Guarantee. It is proposed that during the interim period, the existing Principals of SOC and CSM should act as joint Principals of the new Course.

* *It is proposed that the Course should be named "the South East Institute for Theological Education".*

2) *The South*

34. The proposed Southern Region should primarily cover the Dioceses of Chichester, Guildford, Portsmouth, Salisbury and Winchester and its new Regional Course should be based on the existing Southern Dioceses Ministerial Training Scheme (SDMTS). The area of the five Dioceses is smaller than that covered by SDMTS, which also has Bristol and Bath and Wells within its catchment area. The Steering Group envisages that, in future, these two Dioceses will be involved chiefly in the development of the new South West Region (see paragraph 40). It recognises that for certain candidates from Bristol and Bath and Wells, and also from Guildford and London Dioceses, the access to local tutoring of SDMTS may suit their personal circumstances better than week-night attendance at a teaching centre in their own Dioceses.

35. The Board of SDMTS has formed the nucleus of a forum to discuss how part-time ordination training should be organised in the Region. It has been confirmed by local representatives of the Methodist and United Reformed Churches that the Course meets the ordination training requirements of their Churches. Negotiations are well advanced with a view to the Course's ordination training programme being validated by Southampton University as a Diploma in Christian ministry. Also, staff have been exploring the scope for drawing on the resources of the University of Sussex, King Alfred's College, Winchester and the West Sussex Institute of Higher Education (WSIHE), particularly for student study skills and the training of tutors.

36. The Steering Group had hoped that the Course might have been able to open a teaching centre in, for example, Southampton as an alternative to students working in small tutorial groups. However the SDMTS Board considers that there would be insufficient numbers to justify this and have only been able to suggest mounting study days on specific themes. The Steering Group believes that the option of teaching centres, already admitted in the case of students taught at Chichester, should be reconsidered from time to time, in the hope that it might become a significant feature in the experience of all students on the Course.

37. To broaden the management of the Course, representatives of the Methodist Church, Southampton University and WSIHE are to join the Governing Body. (The URC already has a representative on it).

38. Salisbury and Wells Theological College is currently the main institutional resource for the Course, providing residential accommodation; professional staff to write teaching units and lead seminars; shared use of common room facilities, library and bookshop; and administrative back-up. Nevertheless, the Course is largely independent of the College and could obtain such resources from other institutions in the Region.

39. The Steering Group is concerned that the Course should rebuild its association with Chichester Theological College. At one time, this involved joint staffing, with some Course activities taking place in the College. The Principal of Chichester Theological College would welcome increased cooperation between the two institutions and his membership of the SDMTS Board should facilitate this development.

3) *The South West*

40. The South West region spans the Dioceses of Hereford, Gloucester, Bristol, Bath and Wells, Exeter and Truro. A forum has been discussing how part-time ordination training can best be organised throughout the Region. Representation on the forum has included the Gloucester School for Ministry* (GSM), the South West Ministerial Training Course (SWMTC), the Methodist and United Reformed Churches, Bristol and Bath and Wells Dioceses, and Trinity and Wesley Colleges in Bristol.

41. Although the Steering Group hopes that the current development will lead ultimately to a single unified Course for the whole Region, it accepts that such an objective is more likely to be achieved by a gradual growing together of the existing institutions rather than by an attempt to establish a new organisation that does not evolve naturally from the present provision. It has therefore agreed that the

* *From 1st September 1992, the Gloucester School for Ministry changed its name to West of England Ministerial Training Course.*

Governing Bodies of GSM and SWMTC should continue, but that there should be one Regional Board of Studies with specifically delegated powers. The South West Bishops and the two Governing Bodies have agreed that these should include:

- drawing up a syllabus and a common submission under the ACCM 22 procedure;

- advising GSM and SWMTC on the staffing and financial implications of the agreed syllabus;

- creating, from the detailed budgets of GSM and SWMTC, a single budget for submission to the ABM (these budgets would have taken account also of local requirements for the training of, for example, Readers and LNSM);

- identifying resources available in the Region and commissioning special resources where appropriate (eg. distance learning materials);

- coordinating the planning of residential periods and joint Summer Schools.

It is envisaged that the Region will have teaching centres in Bristol (starting in September, 1992) and Taunton in addition to those currently operated at Gloucester and Ludlow by GSM and at Exeter, Truro and sometimes Plymouth by SWMTC. The Bristol centre is being coordinated by a development officer based in Wesley College and funded by the Methodist Church. The United Reformed Church has agreed that 40% of the time of its local Training Officer can be devoted to the Taunton Centre. Amendment of the Governing Bodies of GSM and SWMTC is under consideration to reflect ecumenical links and to give representation to the Dioceses of Bristol and Bath and Wells.

4) *Oxford, St Albans and London Dioceses*

42. The Steering Group recommends that one new Regional Course should serve the Dioceses of Oxford, St Albans and London, operating through several teaching centres. Although, at first sight, this might appear to be too wide an area to be covered by one

Course, it is in fact no larger than that already successfully covered by the Northern Ordination Course (NOC) through its teaching centres in Chester, Manchester and Leeds. The size of the catchment area makes NOC both educationally and financially viable and the strong body of staff which it is able to support carries academic credibility. The Steering Group sees the same advantages accruing to an Oxford/St Albans/London Regional Course.

43. This is a Region rich in theological resources. It has within it or nearby the Universities of Oxford, London and Surrey, the three Church of England Theological Colleges in or near Oxford, Oak Hill College, Baptist, Methodist and URC Colleges and Roman Catholic religious houses in Oxford, the Roehampton Institute which includes RC, Anglican and Methodist Colleges, Heythrop College and Allen Hall (both RC), Spurgeon's Baptist College, the London Bible College, All Nations Christian College, the Urban Learning Foundation in East London and the Simon of Cyrene Theological Institute.

44. The Region is currently served by the Oxford Ministry Course (OMC), the St Albans Diocese Ministerial Training Scheme (SADMTS) and the Oak Hill Ministerial Training Course (OHMTC). The latter, with its particular theological stance, draws candidates from a wide area both within and outside London. The strategy developed by the Steering Group, from the House of Bishops' endorsement of ACCM 30 recommendations, would mean that the three Courses should together form a single Regional Course. OHMTC has been unwilling to do this and has looked to offer its own Course to the Dioceses of London and Chelmsford. Because of its particular theological stance, it would however be unworkable for OHMTC to have virtually exclusive responsibility for a geographical area. It would similarly be inappropriate for OHMTC, without a region, to draw candidates from the catchment areas of several Regional Courses thus reducing their breadth and weakening their viability. It would, on the other hand, be desirable for OHMTC to add its distinctive contribution to those of the OMC and SADMTS in establishing a new Regional Course, equally acceptable to the Church of England and to the Methodist and United Reformed Churches (OHMTC is not currently recognised by the Methodist Church).

45. Such a new Regional Course would, naturally, be subject to the flexibility of boundaries referred to in paragraph 28 above (eg. a number of candidates from Chelmsford Diocese might be best suited by attendance at a teaching centre in north east London), but the Steering Group wishes to emphasise that such flexibility should depend only on geographical convenience and the personal circumstances of candidates and should not be allowed to extend to theological issues. All the new Courses must be acceptable across the whole range of theological views present in all the sponsoring Churches.

46. The existing Courses vary considerably in numerical strength (see Appendix C). OMC has strengthened its base of Anglican ordination candidates, but has no students from other Churches. SADMTS, while having a strong base of students concerned in lay training, has very few sponsored ordination candidates. OHMTC scarcely satisfies the size criterion for ordination candidates and, under the new pattern of Courses, with Chelmsford making a strong contribution to EAMTC, Rochester structurally involved with the new South-East Theological Course and candidates able to cross boundaries only for exceptional reasons, will be likely to have a smaller base of ordination candidates in future.

47. Following an initial meeting with representatives of the three Courses, the Steering Group asked them to prepare a vision for one organisation covering the Region, indicating how all three Courses could make their particular contributions, allowing even greater variety of teaching (both in content and style), church tradition and theological approach, and more mutual support for staff than might be possible under the existing arrangements.

48. The Courses have so far made only partial progress towards the objective outlined by the Steering Group. They have felt that the proposed new Region is too large and have therefore pursued the alternative of two Courses, one a merger of Oxford and St Albans, the other a Course based on OHMTC. They suggest that representatives of these two Courses would meet together periodically, with representatives of the Dioceses concerned and the other Churches, in a Colloquium.

49. The staffs of OMC and SADMTS have agreed a common philosophy for their new Course and a procedure for union. They will shortly be preparing a joint ACCM 22 proposal and addressing staffing and financial issues. The new Course is planned to begin operating in September 1994 from two outlets, one in Oxford and the other possibly in Luton. There is to be a joint meeting of the existing governing bodies of OMC and SADMTS in October 1992 to set up a provisional joint governing body for the new Oxford/St Albans Course and a Board of Studies. The Group welcomes this development.

50. Although OHMTC has been represented at the discussions for the new Oxford/St Albans Course, it has been pursuing independently its own plans for a Course based on London and Chelmsford Dioceses. No proposals have yet been put forward. Doubts have already been expressed above as to whether such a Course could be numerically viable. The Steering Group believes that the restrictive nature of the Kingham Hill Trust Deed makes it very unlikely that a Course based solely on Oak Hill and dependent on the Kingham Hill Trustees could satisfy the requirements for ordination training across the whole spectrum of the Church of England and command the approval of the Methodist and United Reformed Churches. This was one of the compelling reasons why the Steering Group reached the conclusion that, if Oak Hill was to continue to make a contribution to part-time theological training, it must be in the context of Oak Hill making its distinctive contribution as part of a more broadly based Course.

51. If the Steering Group's objective of one Course for the whole Oxford/St Albans/London Diocese Region does not prove attainable, then two closely-linked Courses with a common ACCM 22 submission and common Board of Studies might be an acceptable, albeit second-best, alternative. A Colloquium of the type mentioned in paragraph 48 would be quite inadequate. Under an arrangement for two closely-linked Courses, the Steering Group envisages that the needs of London Diocese and London-oriented candidates from Chelmsford would need to be met by a new Course, sponsored by London Diocese in association with Chelmsford and based on a teaching centre in central London to which, subject to its future role, Oak Hill might make a contribution.

52. This question of the provision for London Diocese needs determination by the House of Bishops and detailed follow-up by the monitoring group which is proposed in paragraph 225 below.

5) *The Midlands*

53. This section of the Report discusses the Region currently served by the West Midlands Ministerial Training Course (WMMTC) and the East Midlands Ministry Training Course (EMMTC). The WMMTC covers at present the Dioceses of Lichfield, Birmingham, Worcester, Coventry and Peterborough; the EMMTC covers Leicester, Derby, Southwell and Lincoln.

54. The two Courses have sprung from very different origins and this has strongly affected their nature. WMMTC began as an offshoot of the Queen's College, Birmingham. Although it is now relatively independent of the College, it is constitutionally linked to the College Council and relies heavily on the College's facilities. Queen's is the Course's only teaching centre and it provides library, chapel, seminar rooms and residential accommodation for WMMTC. The College also gives administrative support to the Course. Hitherto, WMMTC has been exclusively aimed at part-time ordination training and this has apparently been its attraction for the Diocese of Peterborough, despite the extremely expensive and time-consuming travel for such candidates on week-nights. The Course is now exploring ways in which it can diversify, consistent with its primary purpose, by making contributions to lay education and to the in-service training of the clergy. It is also seeking validation from the Department of Theology of the University of Birmingham as a Diploma in Practical Theology.

55. EMMTC is based on and sponsored by the Adult Education Department of the University of Nottingham. For that reason, it must be open not only to ordination candidates but also to lay students seeking theological education. This had led to difficulty in providing a strong enough focus for ordination training and in securing a satisfactory balance between ordinands and lay students in the composition of year groups. Nevertheless, the Course has been valued for its model of ordinands and lay students training side by side and it has strong representation on its council not only from the four sponsoring dioceses but also from the Methodist and United Reformed Churches. The strong cadre of "private" lay students on

EMMTC has led to the need for a differential fee structure, with the fee for private students being at a much lower level than that for ordination candidates, although both benefit from the same staff input and quantity of training. Without this low fee for private students, sufficient would not be attracted and sponsorship by the Adult Education Department could not be sustained. This has given a problem to the ABM Finance Committee and to the other Churches, since they have to be assured that the balance of cost of training for the private students is met from other income generated by the Course and is not subsidised by funds intended to support ordination training. The Steering Group is not convinced that this has always been achieved. It could be that transfer of sponsorship to the Department of Theology at Nottingham, who already moderate student work for the Course, would make the recruitment of private candidates less critical for the survival of the Course and so simplify its finances. The Steering Group believes that this should be explored by EMMTC in conjunction with the ABM.

56. Despite the differences of origin of the two Courses, the Steering Group's view is that there is much to be gained from regarding the Midlands as one Region and encouraging ever closer co-operation between the WMMTC and EMMTC. They have, in fact, several points in common:

i) They are both ecumenical in terms of student composition and management structure.

ii) They both operate through teaching centres which are central to their educational approach.

iii) They both have (or are seeking) University validation.

iv) They either make, or are considering making, contributions to lay education.

57. It may be objected that a Region covering nine Dioceses would be too large. That has not been the experience of the Northern Ordination Course which has gained from its wide student base and consequential strength of staffing.

58. As a start to closer co-operation, the Steering Group has asked the two Courses to establish a joint Board of Studies with a view to the preparation of a joint submission under the ACCM 22 procedure. This would ensure that part-time ordination training across the Midlands was based on a common philosophy and curriculum, whilst preserving the facility for local delivery through varied educational models and optional courses. The Group believes that this would result in beneficial cross-fertilisation of good practice, integrated staff development and a stronger staff team. Validation by more than one University need not be a problem and was indeed the case in earlier stages of the development of EMMTC. This development would eliminate the need for candidates to travel further than their nearest teaching centre, whether that were Birmingham, Nottingham or Lincoln and could also help the growth of some local training activities and tutoring to reduce the frequency of week-night travel. It would also act as an insurance against any future diminution in numbers (caused possibly by the attractiveness of the new Open Theological College to private students - see paragraph 121 below) by leaving open the possibility of closer structural integration of the two Courses should this prove necessary in the future. The basis would have been laid and it would not be necessary to set up yet another House of Bishops' Group to consider what should be done in such circumstances.

59. The Steering Group therefore sees the joint Board of Studies and joint ACCM 22 submission as a key development for the Midlands Courses, central to their ability to provide acceptable, accessible and effective courses of ordination training throughout the Region. It strongly recommends that this work should be put in hand without delay. It should be given priority over plans which the two Courses have been considering, which might lead in the longer term to the creation of regional theological institutes in the West and East Midlands. We hope that such longer term developments will be discussed in the context of our proposal for Regional Consortia later in this Report (see paragraphs 217 to 223).

6) *East Anglia*

60. The East Anglian Region covers the Dioceses of Chelmsford, Ely, Norwich and St Edmundsbury and Ipswich. The Steering Group expects, however, that the boundaries of this Region will need to be

interpreted flexibly in both directions, along the lines suggested in paragraph 28. In this instance, some Chelmsford candidates might be more conveniently trained through a new Regional Course with a teaching centre in London, while some candidates from the south of Lincoln or north-east of Peterborough might find the local tutoring arrangements of the East Anglian Ministerial Training Course (EAMTC) more practicable than week-night attendance at a teaching centre in the Midlands.

61. For reasons which the Steering Group fully appreciates, the Council of EAMTC has only recently been able to start the process of developing a new Regional Course for East Anglia. It has now, however, begun discussions with both the Methodist and United Reformed Churches as to the training needs of their candidates. It has also expressed itself as being willing to respond to any requests which the local Dioceses might make for assistance with LNSM or lay training. The East Anglian Course is unlikely ever to be numerically strong, but the extension of its catchment area to cover the majority of Chelmsford candidates and the other developments referred to above should help it to attain some stability.

62. The Council is establishing a small Executive Committee. The Steering Group has asked it to make progress also with setting up a Board of Studies and with developing a formal policy of group (as opposed to one-to-one) tutoring as recommended in the last inspection.

63. The Course is exploring the extent to which it can make fuller use of the resources of the Faculty of Divinity in the University of Cambridge and of other East Anglian Universities, Colleges and Institutes. It is beginning to become more closely related to the Cambridge Federation of Theological Colleges. The Steering Group recommends that EAMTC should seek full membership of the Federation, on an equal footing with Ridley Hall, Wesley House, Westcott House, Westminster College (and the Roman Catholic Lady Margaret Beaufort School of Theology recently founded in Cambridge, which it is understood is also applying for membership). Such a basis of involvement would provide the best impetus for the Course to gain educationally from the Federation and to make its own distinctive contribution to it.

7) *The North*

64. The Northern Region is, in broad terms, the area currently served by the Northern Ordination Course (NOC). It covers the Dioceses of Chester, Liverpool, Manchester, Wakefield and Sheffield and the southern parts of the Dioceses of Blackburn, Bradford, Ripon and York. The boundary between the Northern Region and the Cumbria and North-East Region is a notional line drawn from Lancaster in the west to Bridlington on the east coast (see Appendix R). Our general comments as to the porosity of boundaries (see paragraph 28) apply particularly to this one. The sensible allocation of candidates between the two Regions will depend on good liaison between the Diocesan Directors of Ordinands and the new Regional Courses.

65. Recently the new curriculum for the Northern Ordination Course has provided for the course to be modularised without destroying its integrity. The evening teaching in the three centres at Chester, Manchester and Leeds has been separated from the work being done at weekends. The evenings use the standard theological disciplines (eg. Biblical Studies, Doctrine) whilst the weekends are thematic and ministerial in focus. This has enabled NOC to cooperate with other institutions - Chester College, Manchester University and the University College of Ripon and York St John - for its week-night teaching. The new arrangements give candidates the opportunity of working at either MA, Diploma or Certificate level. The Course is willing to consider similar development at other centres.

66. As a full member of the Northern Federation, NOC is fully involved ecumenically and is, in fact, a tenant of the Northern Baptist College at Luther King House in Manchester. At present, NOC is used by only Anglican and Methodist students, but the possibility is being explored with the Manchester Christian Institute of opening it also to Baptist, URC and Roman Catholic students based on a 50/50 ordinand/lay mix. The Steering Group believes it to be essential that this generally desirable development should not be allowed to detract from the attention required by ordination candidates or lead to differential fee levels.

67. Although NOC has clearly been engaged in much fruitful educational development, this has not been matched by structural change. The Council of NOC is strongly Anglican with only one Methodist

representative and hardly any input from other educational bodies. The balance of the Council's membership needs to be changed to reflect its new role as the governing body of a Regional Course serving not only the Church of England but also other Churches. Similarly, it needs to be backed up by an effective Board of Studies with representation from appropriate educational bodies including Chester College and Leeds University.

8) *Cumbria and the North East*

68. This Region covers the area between the Lancaster-Bridlington line referred to above and the Scottish border (see Appendix R). It embraces the Dioceses of Carlisle, Durham and Newcastle and the northern parts of Blackburn, Bradford, Ripon and York.

69. The Steering Group considers that, as soon as possible, the Region should be covered by one fully-integrated Regional Course, involving not only the existing Carlisle Diocesan Training Institute (CDTI) and North East Ordination Course (NEOC), but also the Wesley Study Centre in Durham.

70. We have been encouraged by the important discussions between the Steering Group and representatives on CDTI and NEOC over the past two years but we are disappointed that, so far, only preliminary steps towards cooperation have been taken. The staff of the two Courses and of the Wesley Study Centre are about to begin to design a new joint curriculum for submission under the ACCM 22 procedure, to strengthen the educational programme from September 1994. The two Councils have agreed in principle to "the eventual appointment" of a joint Board of Studies/Academic Board to be responsible for the common philosophy and the design of the joint curriculum, joint academic accreditation and coordination of joint staff training and development programmes. At the moment the Councils each intend to retain authority over staff policy, budgets and course delivery for their areas. If their objective of September 1994 for implementation of the new educational programme is to be achieved, the joint Board of Studies, with clear delegated responsibilities, will need to be established by not later than March 1993. To harness the best educational resources, it will need to include representatives of Cranmer Hall and of the Universities of Durham, Newcastle and Lancaster and of St Martin's College, Lancaster.

71. These limited commitments are only the beginning of that development towards some form of single Regional Course, "owned" by the Dioceses concerned, which the Steering Group believes necessary for the provision of securely-based ordination training throughout the Region (see recommendations 24 to 37 of ACCM 30 as set out in Appendix B). However devolved the provision of teaching centres and/or local tutors of the Course might be, its work should be the responsibility of one Council whose membership would include representation of all the Dioceses concerned, the Methodist and United Reformed Churches, Cranmer Hall, and local institutions of higher education. The Board of Studies, if it has an appropriate membership, could be the necessary first stage towards that objective. There is still a long way to go, and the Steering Group believes that acceptance of the present position by the House of Bishops should be understood as merely endorsing it as a first stage and that a timetable for the implementation of the final objective in fulfilment of ACCM 30 should be set by the monitoring group (see paragraph 225).

g) Financial Implications of the Proposals

72. The Steering Group has never expected that its review of the arrangements for part-time theological training across England would result in significant cost reductions. The main requirement has been to strengthen the educational viability of parts of the system so that effective delivery of a high quality of training can be available right across the country. The progress described above goes some way towards this goal, but the comments on the stage reached show that, whilst the Group is content with the progress being made in some Regions, it has serious reservations about the pace of development and level of commitment to it in others. It will be a key task for the monitoring group, which is proposed in paragraph 225 below, to ensure that all Regions complete a satisfactory evolution.

73. The ACCM 30 report commented that the finances of the existing Courses were intrinsically unstable in that a sudden drop in student numbers could lead either to an excessively high fee increase or to the need for a grant from the Reserve Fund. As mentioned in paragraph 13 above, it concluded that if, however, a Course were of a sufficient size to be educationally viable it would also be likely to prove financially viable. The Steering Group shares this view.

74. The new Regional Courses are intended to be large enough for student numbers to support an adequate core staff and this will be assisted if, as we recommend, each Course is acceptable to both the Methodist and United Reformed Churches (see paragraph 22(2)). The strength of the core staff will allow training services to be offered to the local Dioceses and this too will benefit the financing of the Course. Although it is not possible to be definitive as to the likely costs involved until the structure of all Regional Courses has been determined in accordance with ACCM 30, the Steering Group expects the ongoing running costs of the new Regional Courses, once fully established, to be at a similar level, per student, to those of the larger existing Courses, even though some of the existing subsidies from particular dioceses may no longer continue.

75. There will in some cases, be a transitional period where a new Course will have strengthened staffing before the flow of candidates from the other Churches has built up and before the charging of Dioceses for training services has started. The Steering Group does not, however, expect such additional transitional costs to be significant. If, in any particular case, the move to a new organisation involves specific additional setting-up costs, the Steering Group believes that these should be covered by a special grant to the new Course from the General Synod training budget, made subject to the prior approval of the ABM Finance Committee. We believe that any setting-up costs should not be reflected in the fee level.

76. Although the new structure will not be in place until the academic year 1994/95, the Steering Group recommends that the ABM Finance Committee should prepare a revised fee application form, on the basis proposed in paragraph 23(vi) above, and invite Courses to complete this for 1993/94 as if the new structure was then in place. This will provide both the Finance Committee and the Courses with an opportunity to see how the new arrangements will work in practice and give time for any amendment to the arrangements and/or form, found necessary as a result of this "trial run", before the formal introduction of the new arrangements for 1994/95.

h) Recommendations

77. In relation to this work which the Steering Group has been carrying out with the Courses, the House of Bishops is invited to:

i) endorse the essential considerations (paragraph 22) and structural characteristics (paragraph 23) developed by the Steering Group;

ii) agree the line of approach currently being recommended for each Region (paragraphs 30-71) and to underline the need for the existing Courses to be fully committed to these developments so that quick progress can be made;

iii) note that the House will be asked formally to recognise each new Regional Course as soon as -

a) its submission under the ACCM 22 procedure has been cleared by the EVSC (paragraph 14.i)),

and

b) the Advisory Board of Ministry has accepted that the proposals for the Course represent an adequate response to the recommendations of ACCM 30 with regard to educational factors, staffing levels and management structure (paragraph 14.ii)),

and

c) the ABM Finance Committee has agreed any special financial arrangements needed to enable the existing Course(s) to move to the new structure (paragraph 75);

iv) agree that the ABM Finance Committee and the Courses should be requested to carry out a "trial run" of a new fee application form for 1993/94, on the new arrangement and as if the new structure was in place, in tandem with the normal fee application process for that year (paragraph 76).

78. Although in some Regions it has not proved possible to complete the agreement of the new arrangements by August 1992 (see paragraph 14), the Steering Group hopes that, in the majority of cases, the process of recognition will be completed by the Autumn of 1993 so that the new Regional Courses can become operational from the 1994-95 academic year. Specific approval by the House of Bishops of the lines of approach being recommended for each Region should provide the required impetus to the

negotiations in those Regions where work still remains to be done, so as to ensure, as far as practicable, that the deadline for full implementation of the ACCM 30 proposals for the 1994/95 academic year is achieved throughout the country.

D. FULL-TIME THEOLOGICAL TRAINING

a) Formation of the Advisory Group

79. In the autumn of 1990, the Committee of ACCM Bishops (now the Bishops' Committee for Ministry) received a report on the number of "sponsored students" training in the Theological Colleges in England. ("Sponsored students" means those candidates sponsored by English Bishops for ordination training or to be trained as accredited lay workers). The report showed that the drop in the number of sponsorships and recommendations for training first apparent in 1988 (see Appendix D) had now translated itself into a significant drop in the number of sponsored students in the Theological Colleges. The Bishops' Allocation* of sponsored students for particular Colleges had already been reduced by 5% overall for the academic year 1990-91. The number of sponsored students in training in October 1990 was 86 below this reduced Bishops' Allocation and 130 below the original. The detailed position at that time is shown below:

*Note: *The Bishops' Allocation sets a ceiling on the number of sponsored students that may be recruited by each Theological College. It is intended to give some protection to the weaker Colleges when there is a dearth of candidates. The Allocation does not include such sponsored students from England as may be trained in Scotland or Wales.*

College	Bishops' Allocation		Sponsored Students in Training	
	Original	**Revised for 1990-91**	**October 1990**	**(October 1989)**
Chichester	52	50	37	(36)
Cranmer Hall	77	73	62	(69)
Lincoln	70	66	51	(53)
Mirfield	40	38	28	(30)
Oak Hill	68	65	60	(59)
Queen's	37	35	30	(21)
Ridley Hall	50	48	48	(52)
Ripon, Cuddesdon	70	66	66	(65)
StJohn's,Nottm	98	93	82	(89)
St Stephen's House	58	55	50	(49)
Salisbury and Wells	72	68	59	(59)
Trinity	79	75	77	(75)
Westcott Hse	47	45	40	(47)
Wycliffe Hall	67	64	65	(66)
	885	841	755	(770)

80. Although the Theological Colleges had been expecting a drop in the number of sponsored students, the position in October 1990 was worse than they had forecast. Half the 14 Colleges had not achieved the overall number of students on which their fee levels had been based; more than half had not achieved the number of sponsored students they had expected from the English dioceses. There was evidence of serious depletion of capital funds in certain Colleges. Financial difficulties had been experienced not only by those Colleges which were short of their Bishops' Allocation, but also, to some extent, by those whose ability to recruit had been restricted by the reduction imposed for 1990-91. There was a real danger that a continued low number of students would seriously weaken the financial position of all the Colleges, not just of some.

81. The situation was aggravated by the need to contain the increase in the General Synod's Training Budget. Fees could not simply be inflated to compensate for lower numbers of students. In addition, expenditure on

urgent unbudgeted major repairs exacerbated operating losses and resulted in the need for loans to certain Colleges from the Theological Colleges and Courses Reserve Fund to cover cash-flow problems. Declining student numbers were leading in some cases to staff cuts. (In other cases, it has not been possible for staff to be reduced. This has made the staff:student ratio too generous and increased per capita costs). For smaller Colleges in particular, staff reductions have put at risk the improvements in the quality of the curriculum and of the training itself which had been achieved through the ACCM 22 procedure.

82. The effect on staff numbers had been noted by the Bishops' Inspectors. As a result, the Bishops' Committee on Inspections had sought the advice of the ACCM Committee for Theological Education as to the minimum level of staffing for a Theological College (see Appendix E). The implication of this advice was that, if overall student numbers fell significantly below 50 in any Theological College, the quality of teaching would be seriously impaired.

83. At the same time, concern had been expressed in the General Synod about the quality and cost of theological training and the question had been asked whether the Church should continue to look to independent Theological Colleges to train its ordained ministry. A number of alternative suggestions had been put forward. These matters were addressed in the meeting between the ABM and the House of Laity in February 1991.

84. In January 1991, the Committee of ACCM Bishops reported to the House of Bishops on the problems facing the Theological Colleges. The House decided to set up an Advisory Group on Full-time Theological Training and it was established in April 1991 by the Standing Committee of the House with the following terms of reference and membership:

Terms of Reference

i) To suggest an overall strategy for theological training involving both Colleges and Courses.

ii) To gather facts about the capacity of each Theological College* to meet the basic educational and financial criteria required in an institution providing full-time ordination training, as described in the Annex to Paper HB(91)5**.

iii) To consult with other denominations to take account of their needs, plans and resources.

iv) To take account of the theological resources in the Universities and other institutions of Higher Education.

v) To consult with the Governing Bodies and Principals of the existing Theological Colleges.

vi) To take account of the role which Theological Colleges might play in relation to continuing ministerial education and lay training.

vii) To consider to what extent the need for resources might be affected by greater flexibility in the context of training and in the length and patterns of the training year.

viii) To recommend to the House of Bishops by the Summer of 1992 a plan for matching, within the following three years, the capacity of Theological Colleges to the numbers of clergy required for the future, but taking into account also the likely flow of ordination candidates.

* *The Group will need to acknowledge the opportunities for ordination training that exist in other Provinces, such as those at Coates Hall, Edinburgh, and St Michael's College, Llandaff.*

** *This was a paper presented to the House of Bishops. The basic educational and financial factors referred to are set out in Appendix F to this Report.*

Membership

The Rt Revd Robert Hardy, Bishop of Lincoln (Chairman)

The Ven Michael Bourke, Archdeacon of Bedford (Vice-Chairman)

The Revd Michael Dunford, until June 1992 Secretary for Ministerial Training, United Reformed Church

Mr Derek Foster, Chartered Accountant, Treasurer of the Southwark Ordination Course and Financial Adviser to Simon of Cyrene Theological Institute

The Revd Dr John Muddiman, Fellow and Tutor in Theology at Mansfield College in Oxford and Chairman of the Advisory Board of Ministry's Educational Validation Sub-Committee

The Revd John Taylor, General Secretary, Division of Ministries, Methodist Church

The Revd Canon Dr Joy Tetley, Director of Post Ordination Training, Diocese of Rochester

Consultants: The Rt Revd Stephen Sykes, Bishop of Ely

Dr Sinclair Goodlad, Executive Consultant to the Council of Church and Associated Colleges

Staff: The Revd Canon Hugh Marshall (Chief Secretary, ABM)

Mr John Newton - Secretary (formerly Administrative Secretary, ACCM/ABM)

The Revd Dr Brian Russell (Secretary to IMEC)

b) The Process

85. In deciding how to set about its task, the Advisory Group was able to draw on the educational and financial information on the Theological Colleges held by the ABM. This enabled the Group to identify those areas in which it needed more information, or where it wished to check on details of the received wisdom. It lead to the compilation of a questionnaire which Principals were asked to complete in June, 1991. The questionnaire covered the following topics:

- Numbers and categories of students.
- Teaching staff.
- Links with universities and the Council for National Academic Awards (CNAA).
- Links with other educational bodies, including part-time Theological Courses, Colleges of other denominations and Church Colleges of Higher Education.
- Other resources available in the region.
- Links with dioceses.
- The College as a resource to its region and to the wider Church.
- Plans for contraction, expansion or change in the pattern of ordination training.
- The financial situation and future capital needs.
- College premises and accommodation for single and married students and for staff.
- The College's constitution.
- Any other issues which the College wished to raise.

86. In the early autumn of 1991, the Advisory Group held a plenary discussion with the Theological College Principals, attended also by some representatives of the part-time Courses. In the discussion, the Principals offered to submit a paper setting out their overall views on longer-term issues. This was received in February 1992 and is attached as Appendix G.

The Principal of Salisbury and Wells Theological College was concerned that the paper was substantially an argument for maintenance of the status quo with a few modifications and did not take sufficiently seriously the present situation in the Church's ordained ministry and current developments. He wrote instancing several questions which the Advisory Group should address in working out an overall strategy. An extract from his letter is given at Appendix H.

87. Meanwhile, the Advisory Group had received from the College Principals valuable and detailed answers to the questionnaire as it affected their individual institutions. These were discussed in individual meetings usually with the Chairman of the Governing Body and the Principal of each Theological College during the latter part of 1991 and early 1992.

88. At the same time, enquiries were made as to the provision made by other Churches and the Group's Chairman had a useful exploratory meeting with the Chairman's Advisory Group of the Council of Church and Associated Colleges (CCAC). Also a submission was received from the Association of Ordinands and Candidates for Ministry (AOCM).

89. The process of consultation concluded with meetings with representatives of the ABM Finance Committee covering the method of financing Theological Colleges generally, the circumstances of each individual institution and the financial implications of the proposals developed.

90. Throughout this process, the Advisory Group had been identifying issues which needed to be addressed in the short, medium and long term. The objective was not only to deal with the short term problems of the Theological Colleges, but also to develop an overall strategy for theological training in the longer term. A key element in the former was the creation of a set of criteria against which the current 14 Colleges could be assessed. In developing the longer term vision, the Advisory Group met residentially with the Steering Group for Theological Courses to ensure coherence between the aims of the two Groups and the overall recommended strategy.

c) Educational Issues

91. Some of the educational issues identified during this process are of major significance to the future development of the Church's ministry. Some concern both Colleges and Courses; others relate exclusively to the Colleges. They affect the way in which candidates should be prepared for the exercise of that ministry; they suggest how the relationship between theological training and the Universities and Colleges of Higher Education

should develop; and they are significant also for the future supply of theological educators. We have already alluded also (see paragraph 82 and Appendix E) to the minimum level of staffing required for a Theological College. These educational issues, and also the financial issues to which we turn later in this report, have influenced the Advisory Group strongly in formulating criteria for the Theological Colleges of the future (see paragraphs 156 to 159).

1) The Value of Residence

92. As has already been explained in paragraph 6, both Colleges and Courses have elements of "residence" in their training patterns. For Theological Colleges, the pattern of residence for three academic terms a year is largely determined by the need to enable students to benefit from the teaching in University courses. The vacation periods accommodate student placements and leave the staff space for continuing study, curriculum development and contributing to training in the wider Church. For Courses, the ACCM 30 Report set minimum residential requirements for both summer schools and weekends (see Appendix B, Recommendation 2).

93. In November, 1990, ACCM published a Report on Residence in Theological Education (ACCM Occasional Paper No.38) entitled *Residence: An Education*. ACCM Council accepted the view of the Working Party that "residence" was a powerful instrument for the training of the Church's ministers, particularly in relation to ministerial formation through worship, prayer and personal development. The report proposed that each College and Course should conduct a residence audit to evaluate the use of residence in their institution; and ACCM Council planned that a joint consultation should be held in the spring of 1992 to consider responses from this process. Such a Conference was held in May 1992.

94. The Conference strongly endorsed the value of elements of "residence" provided in different ways both by Colleges offering full-time training and by Courses offering part-time training. The Conference recommended various ways in which Colleges and Courses could make the best use of the opportunities of residence. It felt that, when decisions were taken about "residence", the overriding principle should be the need to equip students to fulfil the mission and ministry of the Church. "Residence" was seen to involve a complex range of expectations and opportunities. Amongst these, the Conference noted the following:

i) **Developing Persons for Ministry**

Opportunities for ordinands to develop personally and corporately in readiness to meet the demands of ordained ministry with well founded spiritual lives and pastoral understanding.

ii) **Developing Spiritual Discipline**

Opportunities for regular corporate worship as a cornerstone of spiritual growth and discipline.

iii) **Learning and Working Corporately**

Opportunities to develop skills and understandings of collaborative ministry through experiencing and reflecting on corporate life in a number of different contexts, including that of the College or Course, the home setting, the parish and the work setting.

This involves opportunities for learning how to handle conflict and diversity creatively. It is also necessary to learn and work together as students and as staff through seminars and other forms of group learning. This assists the development of skills in communication, in understanding and in analysing ideas, insights and the experiences of others.

95. For these reasons, the Conference concluded that elements of "residence" were considered indispensable aspects of the theological training provided by both Colleges and Courses. The Advisory Group accepts this conclusion and notes that certain vital benefits which flow from residence in the context of ordination training in a Theological College, or on a part-time Theological Course, would not be derived from a similar residential period at a University or College of Higher Education. In the future, mixed mode training which might be developed through the agency of a Regional Consortium (see paragraph 220 below) may be designed to contain elements of residence following either the College or Course pattern.

2) Size Factors

96. As long ago as 1968, the de Bunsen Report* produced a detailed study of the educational and economic factors which should determine the future policy for the theological training of ordinands. Their basic criteria were

* *Theological Colleges for Tomorrow: Report of a Working Party appointed by the Archbishops of Canterbury and York, February, 1968.*

that for financial and educational viability the optimum size of a College should be 120 students, with 80 as the absolute minimum. They also recommended that Colleges should either be in, or adjacent to, a University, so as to be able to use the resources of University faculties or departments of theology, or should be sufficiently large to employ so wide a range of staff as to enable them to be self-contained.

97. The Advisory Group agrees with the broad thrust of these conclusions. A College needs to be of a size that the number of ordination candidates allows educationally viable courses to be mounted for 3-year degrees, 3-year certificates and 2-year certificates/diplomas. The body of staff should be able to formulate the syllabus and curriculum and to teach the range of subjects required, to provide a variety of viewpoints, to illustrate team work and to form a sufficient body of colleagues for theological and educational debate. In practice, this means that 6 or 7 is the absolute minimum size for an effective staff establishment and that, bearing in mind the accepted staff:student ratio of 1:10 for Theological Colleges (see Appendix E), no College should have fewer than 60 full-time students.

98. Later in this Report we describe how, for the benefit of the Church at large, it is desirable that Theological Colleges should be able to act as educational resources to their Regions. The Advisory Group's consultations with College representatives and the replies to the questionnaire (see paragraph 87) have made it clear that, unless a College has access to a body of 10 or 12 staff, it is unlikely to be able to embrace such a role effectively.

99. The Advisory Group therefore sees 60 full-time students as the absolute minimum size at present for a non-federated Theological College, but believes that the aim should be for an evolution towards units of 100 to 120 students for all Theological Colleges.

3) Guidelines for Colleges and Courses Training Women

100. For several years now, women have attended Bishops' Selection Conferences alongside men and nearly all the Theological Colleges and all of the Courses have trained women for ordination as deacons or to be accredited lay workers. Men and women are now seen as participating together in an ordained ministry.

101. When the Bishops' Guidelines for Colleges and Courses training Women were revised in 1989, the House of Bishops recognised the need to integrate the ordination training of men and women and took a number of practical steps to this end:

i) By ensuring that women with experience as ordained and accredited lay workers serve in an integrated way in the staffing and teaching of each College and Course training women;

ii) By asking that the women serve as illustrations of ministry for the sake of the men in training as well as for the sake of the women, so that the women staff are not seen as providing only pastoral care and supervision for women students but rather are integrated into the whole educational task of the College or Course;

iii) By encouraging women who are potential future theological teachers or staff members, including the encouragement to read for degrees and postgraduate research during their initial theological training;

iv) By setting as a goal for each College training women, that at least 15% of students training for ordained ministry should be women;

v) By encouraging the curriculum to take specific account of women's perspectives so that these may permeate the way in which the whole curriculum is offered.

102. The Advisory Group accepts that, irrespective of the outcome of the current Synodical debate as to women being ordained to the priesthood, men and women will continue to participate together in the ordained ministry of the Church. An institution which does not train women alongside men, in an integrated manner, is thus not preparing men adequately for the ministry which they will be exercising after their ordination. The Group concludes that the implementation of the 1989 Guidelines is an essential factor for *all* Colleges and Courses training for the ordained ministry.

4) Relationship with the Universities

103. The 1983 Report on the Financing of Training (GS(Misc)175) analysed the differences in aim and approach between the academic teaching of theology in Universities and the teaching of theology, as part of a training for ordained ministry, by the Theological Colleges and Courses. The report recognised that it was clearly right for ordinands to make as much use as possible of the academic resources of Universities to the extent that these were relevant to their needs, but concluded that a formal shift of responsibility for ordination training to the Universities was neither practicable nor desirable.

104. This analysis, the Advisory Group believes, still holds good, although developments since 1983 have strengthened the links between the two systems. The General Ministerial Examination gradually fell into disuse and has now ended. There is now no centrally produced syllabus or examination for Church of England ministerial training. In its place, all Colleges and Courses, within ABM Guidelines, devised their own courses of theological training to prepare candidates for the ordained ministry of the Church. The validation of these courses by the EVSC (see paragraph 8 above) has shown that all the Theological Colleges and some Courses have now developed a link with either a University or CNAA* for validation purposes. In many cases this led to a valuable increase in the input from University teaching, but as part of an integrated course of ministerial training rather than as a separate academic component.

105. In the development of these links, there has been a creative tension between the subject teaching traditional in University Departments and the inter-disciplinary approach encouraged initially by the ACCM Committee for Theological Education and now embodied in the validation requirements of the ABM's EVSC. The latter look for not only an inter-disciplinary approach to the more formal learning of academic subjects, but also the integration of placements and pastoral studies. As the recent IMEC paper notes (see Appendix A), a number of Bachelor of Theology degrees which have existed for some years, allow scope for bringing together theory and practice within an overall programme of ministerial training. These are currently being developed further and similar new degrees have been agreed and introduced by a number of Universities. There is, in fact, an encouraging trend for the Universities to be responsive to the needs which the Church has in the training of its ministers.

106. Concurrently, the conversion of a number of University degree courses into modular form presents both opportunities and problems. It makes possible the selection by Colleges and Courses of certain modules to provide elements of the syllabus or to meet the needs of individual candidates in relation to their prior learning and experience. Eventually it will facilitate credit accumulation and transfer which may introduce flexibility, which can be of value in developing new forms of training. However, care must be taken not to upset the balance of the overall curriculum. Where modules are brought in, provision must be made for the separate elements of the course to be integrated with one another. Equally, the needs of the individual must be considered in the context of the required training for the Church's ordained ministry. These two sets of needs should inter-act. On

* *With the demise of CNAA, Colleges are having to look for validation in future to the Universities.*

the one hand there are needs arising from the age, academic qualifications, personal gifts and maturity of the individual. On the other, the curriculum must satisfy the requirements of the Ordinal for the individual to have a knowledge of the Scriptures, to understand the doctrine of the Christian faith as received by the Church of England and to be equipped to expound and teach it. Response to individual needs, though important, must not therefore be taken so far as to disrupt the integration of the overall pattern of ministerial training.

107. These developments are being closely monitored by IMEC and its Educational Validation Sub-Committee through the ACCM 22 procedure. The Advisory Group finds this increasing inter-relationship between the Universities and the Colleges/Courses encouraging and believes that the future development of these trends, within appropriate parameters, is an essential element in the future theological training of ordinands.

108. In a discussion of these issues with the Advisory Group, the Bishop of Ely pointed out that the Church needs access to a range of University courses so as to allow both those with high educational potential and candidates of average attainment to participate in University education. This is catered for, the Group believes, by a combination of the developments referred to above and the provision for potential theological educators referred to later in this report (see paragraphs 110-113).

109. The Bishop of Ely also drew attention to the need for high quality staff in the Theological Colleges and Courses to foster and operate these University links. In the Advisory Group's conversations with Principals, we were impressed to learn of the contribution already being made by College and Course staff as teachers on University courses. The encouragement of such cross-fertilisation between theological training and University education will benefit both systems.

5) Potential Theological Educators

110. On several occasions, our attention has been drawn to the dearth of theological educators and to the need for the Church to be pro-active both in fostering those with potential in this area and in ensuring that the supply of theologians in the Universities is maintained. Indeed these problems are referred to specifically by the Principals in their paper (see Appendix G, Section 5).

111. The Advisory Group was glad to learn that, in the academic year 1990-91, the ABM had mounted an initiative, which included the creation of a Further Degrees Panel to encourage ordination candidates judged to be

potential theological teachers or educators. The ABM has asked Dioceses, Colleges and Courses to be alert to recognise where current ordination candidates show evidence of being potential theological teachers and to make proposals for them to carry out postgraduate research during their training. The Panel assesses applications from ordinands wishing to carry out such research in subjects suited for equipping them to take part in the Church's formal teaching ministry. (Appendix I shows the criteria used by the Panel in their assessments). In addition, a number of men and women, with similar potential, have been encouraged to read for a first degree in theology in cases where they would not have qualified under the Bishops' Regulations.

112. During the academic year 1989-90, ten ordinands were undertaking higher degrees in theology as part of their ministerial training. Since the summer of 1990, 42 ordinands have been assisted, including 23 for M.Phil, M. Litt or Ph.D degrees. Five of these ordinands were women. Academic subjects have included Biblical Studies, Christian Doctrine and Ethics, Pastoral Theology and, less frequently, Christian Worship, Church History, Christian Education and Spirituality. For some candidates, the proposal has involved permitting an increase in the length of training, funded wherever possible by a British Academy Award.

113. We consider it essential that every Theological College should be staffed sufficiently strongly to be able to encourage such candidates and supervise them where appropriate. We recognise, however, that for some specialist subjects such as liturgy and worship there are likely to be only a few possible sources in England for postgraduate research. In such cases, candidates may need to be encouraged to choose a particular Theological College which, together with the local university, can provide this expertise.

114. There is also a need to encourage potential theological educators who are laity or serving clergy. The Central Fund for Ministerial Training (the General Synod Training Budget) can only be used towards the cost of training for ordination and accredited lay work. Laity and serving clergy cannot be funded from this source. The trust funds from closed Church Colleges of Education occasionally assist in these cases, but are more likely to be devoted to assisting those directly involved in teaching Religious Education in schools. There has also been some scope for assistance from the trust funds and private income (eg. conference income) of Theological Colleges and Courses. Nevertheless, a further source of funding potential theological educators who are laity or serving clergy is still needed urgently. We suggest that some of the funds that might accrue from the closure of a Theological College might be established as a trust, in the name of that College, to be available for grants in such cases. This could include the

possibility of establishing full-time research tutorships or fellowships at Theological Colleges for serving clergy, especially if the individuals would be likely to gain a British Academy Award to assist with their research costs. It would seem convenient and equitable for the trust to be administered by the Further Degrees Panel of the ABM.

6) The Role of Church Colleges of Higher Education

115. The 1983 Report on the Financing of Training discussed also the relationship between ordination training and the Church Colleges of Higher Education (pages 48-51 and Appendix D of that Report). It examined three possibilities:

   i) that ordinands should in future be trained in CCHE's, whose staffs would work side-by-side with Theological College staff;

   ii) that CCHE's might take over the responsibility for providing part of the training only;

   iii) that CCHE's might contribute increasingly to developing the resources available in individual regions to meet the need for theological training of all kinds, including direct cooperation with Theological Colleges.

116. That Working Party felt that the last possibility could be a valuable extension of CCHE activities where they were conveniently situated in relation to Theological Colleges and could offer complementary academic resources. The Working Party concluded that the first two possibilities were not practicable at present. The Advisory Group believes that these conclusions are still valid in the current situation.

117. At the November 1990 session of the General Synod, the question was raised whether greater use should be made of CCHE's in ordination training. It was argued that there would be a financial saving as degree courses offered by the CCHE's attract Local Education Authority (LEA) mandatory awards. The ACCM Grants Secretary advised that it was not clear that there would be any such financial advantage. "The vast majority of ordinands (approximately 73%) are not eligible for mandatory awards because they have previously undertaken a degree or other course of advanced further education of more than two years, and it is the non-graduate category of ordinands who are already most favourably considered by LEA's for discretionary awards for Theological College training..... Furthermore, an additional period of training would be necessary following

any course undertaken at a CCHE in order to fulfil ordination requirements."

118. In our Chairman's discussion with the Chairman's Advisory Group of the CCAC, it was accepted that it would be inadvisable for any CCHE to attempt to set up a new degree course, related to ordination training, without detailed consultation about the disposition of scarce resources. (Such a proposal had recently been made by St Martin's College, Lancaster, but it had not found support from the ABM, nor could the Advisory Group believe that it was appropriate in the present circumstances). The Group agreed, however, with the CCAC's view that there was nevertheless considerable scope for other forms of cooperation between the two systems.

119. Dr Sinclair Goodlad subsequently provided a paper, together with detailed supportive information, describing the work of the CCHE's and giving his views as to possible areas for collaboration. The paper is attached as Appendix J. The Advisory Group on Full-Time Theological Training accepts that there could be fruitful collaboration between Theological Colleges and the CCHE's in the areas suggested by Dr Goodlad:

- Sharing of services of teaching staff.
- Shared library facilities.
- Associate membership for ordinands of CCHE common rooms.
- Shared use of residential facilities.
- Shared teaching facilities.
- Shared technical services.
- Shared insights on models of professional formation.
- Interweaving of professional practices.

120. Cooperation already exists in a number of these areas; the Advisory Group hopes that the longer-term development of Regional Consortia (see paragraphs 217 to 223 below) will give fresh impetus to such collaboration.

7) *Response to Developments in British Education*

121. British education is currently moving through a period of radical change, not only in structures, where there are changes in the established boundaries between Universities, Polytechnics and Colleges of Higher Education and where the demise of CNAA has major implications, but also in educational techniques. Several Universities and Polytechnics have been introducing modular structures for their degree courses. Some institutions are linking this to an academic year comprising two semesters each of 15 weeks rather than the traditional three terms. In a recent initiative, seven Christian Colleges (including three Anglican Theological Colleges) have

combined as "The Open Theological College" to offer a distance learning degree in theology; the course modules are at 3 levels: certificate, diploma and degree. The development of modular structures for courses, enabling these not only to provide elements of the syllabus, but also to be tailored more closely to students' individual needs, brings the danger, in the field of vocational training, of the course of study becoming too student-focused to the detriment of the overall vocational purpose of the course (see paragraph 106). Nevertheless, provided that this tendency is avoided, modularity can enable proper regard to be paid to the prior certificated learning and experience of students. This has led to more formalised assessment of prior learning and, in higher education, the systematisation of credit accumulation and transfer schemes (CATS).

122. The Advisory Group believes that it is important for Theological Colleges and Courses to be aware of and to respond to these developments to the extent that is appropriate for vocational training. Colleges and Courses should be organised to assess, at the outset of training, what candidates have already learnt, what skills and experience they have already acquired and how these relate to what is expected of a candidate for the ordained ministry. Their courses must therefore be sufficiently flexible to respond to the results of such profiling of candidates. (For example, more advanced modules would be appropriate for theology graduates). The courses will also need to give space for students to think through how they can apply their previous knowledge and skills to their future work in the ordained ministry.

123. The external validation of the courses of study offered at Theological Colleges and by the part-time Theological Courses will bring also a valuable spin-off. It will define what "credits" candidates have accumulated during their ordination training and thus make it easier for degrees or certificates/diplomas to be completed or built-on during continuing ministerial education. Such CME might take the form either of the completion of first degrees or the pursuit of postgraduate qualifications.

8) Theological Colleges as Regional Resources

124. Theological Colleges have traditionally been regarded as national institutions. They draw their sponsored students from all dioceses of the Church of England and, in some cases from other provinces in the United Kingdom and overseas. In addition, certain of the Colleges recruit a significant number of students from other Churches and of private students, attracted largely by the College's theological ethos rather than its location. Nevertheless, in recent years, a number of Colleges have offered specialist support to their local dioceses on aspects of continuing ministerial

education and lay training. Although this is not an essential part of a College's role as an institution with the primary aim of ordination training the Advisory Group believes that there are valid and significant reasons for such a development. Theology is not just a discipline required for professional ministry, but a resource needed by the Church at every level of its life. Access to theological resources should therefore, in principle, be opened up as widely as possible, not least for the sake of the future direction of theology itself. The Church cannot afford to duplicate scarce educational resources and so it makes good sense for those of the Theological Colleges to be made available to strengthen the training activities of dioceses in the immediate Region. It can also be of some financial advantage to the Colleges.

125. In developing criteria, against which to assess the current value of individual Colleges, we have therefore seen willingness to act as a regional resource as a desirable feature though not, strictly speaking, essential at this stage. For the longer term, however, we see this as a vital area for development for every College and Course; we shall return to this theme again later in the Group's Report (see paragraphs 217 to 223).

d) Financial Issues

126. The preceding section of this Report draws together several educational issues which have informed the Advisory Group's approach to the type of theological training that the Church of England needs to provide for its ordinands. Before translating these factors into more formal criteria for Theological Colleges, we turn to a number of parallel financial issues.

1) The Status of Theological Colleges

127. As has been observed in previous reviews of theological training, the Theological Colleges have their origin in local and voluntary enterprise. This is reflected in their continuing status as legally-independent and self-governing societies; their survival as institutions is not determined by the Church of England or any other external authorities. The House of Bishops does however "recognise" each institution for the purpose of training sponsored candidates for its ordained ministry. "Recognition" carries with it the obligation to receive educational validation from the ABM and to satisfy the Bishops' Inspectors as to the standard of training, the effectiveness of ministerial formation and the adequate preparation of candidates to exercise ministry in the Church of England. "Recognition" of a College qualifies those of its students sponsored by English Bishops to receive grants from Synod funds; consequently the level of fees charged needs the agreement of the ABM Finance Committee. Thus, although the

House of Bishops cannot decide to "close" a Theological College, withdrawal of recognition would have a serious (and, in some cases, terminal) financial effect, since sponsored students would no longer qualify to receive such grants. In any case where closure resulted, there would however be no guarantee that the Church would continue to benefit from the assets of these institutions for any new ordination training purposes that it wished to introduce.

2) *Method of Financing Theological Colleges*

128. In the main, the finances of the Colleges are organised on the basis that the founding trust is responsible for providing the College premises, while the central Church pays for the annual running costs (both tuition and maintenance) of its sponsored students. This leaves the College with the responsibility of providing capital for new development, whether this be for the extension of teaching facilities or for increased single or married accommodation. (For a few years this responsibility was lightened when the Church Commissioners were able to make available to Colleges equity-sharing loans which provided capital for the purchase of staff and married student housing. This facility has, however, now been withdrawn because of the current financial constraints affecting the Commissioners). The supply of new capital therefore remains the responsibility of the Colleges and can place a heavy burden on Principals (see Appendix G, Section 6.1). As long as Colleges remain independent institutions, it is difficult to see how this situation could be changed, except to the extent that the Church Commissioners might, in a more favourable financial climate, be asked to make their equity-sharing loans available to Colleges once more.

129. The method adopted by the ABM for paying the annual running costs of sponsored students at Theological Colleges is to require all Colleges to submit a fee application early each year, which includes a budget of expected outgoing for the forthcoming academic year, an estimate of sundry income and a forecast of the number of students that will be in training. The object usually is for the College to seek to achieve a break-even position, by applying a fee per student arrived at by dividing the outgoings, less sundry income, by the expected number of students.*

* *Some income and costs are disregarded in this calculation. As regards income, no account is taken of 80% of the profits from conference lettings; similarly, donations, bequests and profits from other activities of the College are disregarded. For costs, depreciation on College premises is excluded, as the premises are not owned by the central Church.*

130. The fee application also gives details of the actual results achieved for the previous academic year (supported by audited accounts) and an updated forecast for the current year. The fee application forms require the costs to be broken down in considerable detail under the following main headings: academic, administrative, catering, household and premises. By analysing these costs and comparing them, on a per capita basis, with those of other Theological Colleges, the ABM Finance Committee is able to see that the Church is not overcharged for the services provided and conversely that, **given the expected flow of candidates**, the College is likely to remain in a financially healthy state.

131. Because the method of financing is per capita, the number of students, both sponsored and other, that a College is able to attract is crucial for its finances. If a College achieves more students than budgeted, it is likely to make a profit; whereas if there are fewer students than expected (and this has been the recent experience) the College will make a loss, unless it can cut its costs rapidly or generate income through some other source of students or type of activity.

3) Recent College Financial Results and their Effect

132. In carrying out its scrutiny of the fee applications over the past three years, the ABM Finance Committee has been particularly aware of pressure from the General Synod for economy in the Training Budget. It has looked very closely at the expected number of students on which the applications have been based and at levels of proposed expenditure. As a result, the fee level applied for by most Colleges has been reduced (except for 2 for 1990/91, 1 for 1991/92 and 6 for 1992/93). The reasons for these reductions have varied from College to College, but include increases in the expected number of students and suggestions for reductions in certain costs and for increases in certain non-fee income. (The actual fees set for the 5 years to 1992/93 are shown at Appendix K).

133. In the event most Colleges have made losses for ABM purposes in each of the three years 1988/89, 1989/90 and 1990/91. The College results for those years, calculated for ABM purposes, are shown in Appendix L. Mirfield has been shown as making neither a profit nor a loss, because the loss on training students arises, to a large degree, due to its fee being substantially lower than those for other Colleges; in effect, it is subsidised by income from the substantial investments owned by the College. As will be seen from Appendix L total College losses for 1988/89 amounted to £218,522, for 1989/90 to £306,567 and for 1990/91 to £356,903. Preliminary indications are that a further substantial aggregate loss will be incurred in 1991/92, although hopefully it will not be as large as for 1990/91. Even

though some of the College losses were largely budgeted for, the results set out in Appendix L are very disturbing. One reason why Colleges have incurred losses rather than break-even is that student numbers have been lower than expected and it has not been possible to reduce costs to compensate for this fall in income.

134. Another reason for some Colleges incurring losses has been the incidence of major repairs, which often have not been anticipated and budgeted in advance. All Colleges are encouraged to set aside amounts for future major repairs when preparing their fee application, but many have not been able to do so because of other restraints on their budget. Accordingly the cost of major repairs has tended to fall in the year in which the expenditure has been incurred, rather than being spread over a number of years. In certain cases, ABM has arranged short term loans to cushion the financial cost of making major repairs (see paragraph 144), but this is only a temporary relief unless the cost of those repairs can be recovered by making profits in subsequent years.

135. Some Colleges have been able to mitigate the effect of these losses by attracting other income (see footnote to paragraph 129), but, even after this, the overall position of Colleges has been to incur losses in each of these three years, although some Colleges have inevitably fared far worse than others. In any event the reason that ABM excludes such other income when determining student fees is to encourage Colleges to maximise such income, to provide them with funds to meet their need for capital. This purpose is negated if such income is used to offset losses on student training.

136. The effect of these losses has been to put a severe strain on the financial resources of many of the Colleges. Only two Colleges (Mirfield and Queen's) have a substantial investment portfolio that could be used to meet any revenue shortfall. Such investments, other than investments in restricted trust funds, that other Colleges may have had in the past have now been virtually exhausted. At the end of the 1990/91 academic year, the highest market value of investments, excluding restricted funds, of any College apart from Mirfield and Queen's was only some £30,000.

137. Some Colleges have been able to realise property to provide funds to meet cash shortfalls due to losses, sometimes by selling houses owned for many years by the College and by purchasing accommodation by means of a fully funded Church Commissioners' equity sharing loan. With the withdrawal of the Church Commissioners scheme and the present depressed state of the property market, it is less likely that College finances will improve due to these factors in the future. In any event, few if any of the Colleges have

property that is surplus to their requirements and any sale of houses would be likely to result in their having to rent accommodation for staff and students instead.

138. In the short term, unforeseen losses are met in the following ways:

i) out of existing reserves (but these are now largely exhausted);

ii) by making use of provisions set aside to finance future major repairs;

iii) by using income from other activities (but this limits the ability of the College to create its own source of capital);

iv) by obtaining loans from the Central Church Fund (through the ABM Finance Committee) to finance major repairs;

v) by obtaining loans or grants from the Theological Colleges and Courses Reserve Fund or elsewhere.

In the long term, however, such losses undermine the financial stability of a College unless they are balanced by profitable years.

139. If a College incurs a loss, this leads to a reduction in its cash resources and, if such losses continue over a period, its ability to continue in existence will be threatened. Appendix M sets out the working capital of each of the Colleges at the date that they respectively made up their accounts in the summer of 1989, 1990 and 1991. The working capital comprises the net current assets/(liabilities), the investments at market value, excluding restricted funds, less loans (other than Church Commissioners equity sharing loans) and any provision for major repairs that the College has been able to put aside. Net current assets comprise the bank and cash balances, debtors and prepayments and stock of the College, less its bank overdraft and creditors and loans due within one year. If the amount is negative there are net current liabilities. The principal assets of a College - its College building and plant and houses owned by the College - have been excluded from the calculation of working capital as these, in the main, could not be realised without undermining the whole operation of the College; as houses have been excluded it is appropriate to exclude also equity sharing loans secured on those houses, since any surplus on ultimate realisation does not accrue to the College.

140. The working capital of a College should show a positive figure since a negative amount would indicate that the College could only discharge its liabilities by realising some of its property, which as stated above is unlikely

to be a viable alternative. Having a negative working capital does not necessarily mean that a College has an immediate financial problem, since the deficit might be due to a loan not due for repayment for many years. However, any deficit in working capital can only be made good by earning profits in the future, receiving donations or realising property. As will be seen from Appendix M, ten of the fourteen Colleges had, in the summer of 1991, a deficit on working capital, six of them having deficits in excess of £50,000.

141. Another reason for a College having a deficit in working capital, apart from losses arising over a number of years, has been the effect of new building work or expenditure on housing not financed through a Church Commissioners equity sharing loan. As stated in paragraph 128, Colleges are responsible for providing and financing premises; a number of them have had to expend quite considerable funds in recent years in making their premises suitable for present conditions. Since few Colleges have financial reserves sufficient for this purpose, these new works have had to be funded by appeals for donations. As it is time consuming to attract such funds, it has frequently been the position that the College has had to proceed with the building work before the funds were assured, leaving the College to bridge the gap by arranging for loans. These loans inevitably place a considerable strain on the working capital of the College.

142. Appendix N sets out a breakdown of the working capital of Colleges at the date to which they respectively made up their accounts in the summer of 1991. It will be seen from this that four Colleges had quite substantial long-term loans outstanding then, details of which are:

i) The loan of £150,000 to Ripon College, Cuddesdon (together with a bank loan of £100,000 included in the net current liabilities) has been made to assist with the financing of the recently built new accommodation block, which it is hoped will be repaid out of the proceeds of an appeal to finance this work.

ii) The loans of £132,061 to Trinity College are housing mortgages not taken out under the Church Commissioners equity sharing loan scheme.

iii) The loans of £165,500 to Lincoln have been made to assist this College refurbish its premises from a weak financial position, and include loans from the Theological Colleges and Courses Reserve Fund and from the Fund to assist finance major repair work (see paragraph 144).

iv) St Stephen's House has a loan of £67,191 from ACOCF.

143. Seven Colleges had, in the summer of 1991, set aside a reserve for future major repairs, but these reserves are not necessarily a fair reflection of the likely cost of such work in the immediately following years, even on the basis of known work that needs to be carried out - and there is always the unexpected work as well (see paragraph 134). To the extent that a College has not made provision, or has not made an adequate provision, its working capital position is flattered and its profits and financial position will suffer when the repairs have to be carried out.

144. As stated in paragraph 138, Colleges can obtain loans from the Central Church Fund to assist with financing major repairs and from the Theological Colleges and Courses Reserve Fund to assist with a short-term financial problem. At 30th June, 1992, outstanding loans to Colleges were:

i) from the Central Church Fund (bearing interest at the CBF deposit rate):

Cranmer Hall	£ 17,032
Lincoln	£ 45,500
Oak Hill	£ 21,000
St John's, Nottingham	£ 24,000
St Stephen's House	£ 6,800
	£114,332

ii) from the Theological Colleges and Courses Reserve Fund (interest free):

Chichester	£ 25,000
Lincoln	£ 10,000
Ridley Hall	£ 15,000
	£ 50,000

145. The Advisory Group has considered carefully the effects of:

i) the losses totalling nearly £900,000 sustained by the Theological Colleges over the last 3 years for which results are available (see paragraph 133);

ii) the prospect of a further substantial aggregate loss for 1991/92 (see paragraph 133);

iii) the difficulty Colleges have experienced in establishing adequate provisions for future major repairs (see paragraph 143);

iv) the deficits on working capital shown by the accounts of ten Colleges in the summer of 1991 (see Appendix M);

v) the loans incurred on new building works (see paragraph 142);

vi) the loans amounting to £164,000 made by the Central Church Fund and the Reserve Fund (see paragraph 144).

One reason for the substantial losses referred to in (i) and (ii) above, which have to a large extent caused the problems referred to in (iii), (iv) and (vi) above is that there are currently too few students using too much plant. The Advisory Group has therefore reached the inescapable conclusion that the overall number of Theological Colleges needs to be reduced so that the continuing Colleges can operate much nearer to their total student capacity.

146. In considering how to achieve this objective, the Advisory Group has concluded that, whilst "market forces" are an important factor, they should not be allowed to determine the outcome. This would be unsound both theologically and educationally. The Church has the responsibility of making the best use of the resources committed to its stewardship. For a College to cease to operate simply because it has recently experienced financial difficulties would leave the balance and quality of educational provision to chance and could lead to both unexpected and undesirable results. We have therefore tried to take into account the educational potential of each institution and to consider the likely financial effect on certain institutions of others no longer competing with them for the available students. We discuss these issues again later in our report (see paragraph 203).

4) A System of Block Grants to Theological Colleges?

147. Most of the costs of a College do not directly vary with the number of students, at least in the short term. The only costs that automatically vary with the number of students are the cost of placements and, to a limited extent, catering and household costs. College finances are very labour-intensive and staff numbers (with the exception of part-time catering and household staff) cannot easily be varied in the short-term, particularly as academic subject specialisms must continue to be covered (see Appendix E).

148. It has been put to us by the Principals that Colleges would have more financial stability if their budgets were divided between fixed and variable costs and if the former were met by a block grant to each College based on its particular circumstances and assessed quinquennially, after a visit to the premises by members of the ABM Finance Committee (See Appendix G, Section 6).

149. In our consultations with the ABM Finance Committee, which is responsible for administering the Synod's training budget, we raised this matter. The Committee sees no advantages in moving to a block grant system of funding for Colleges either in order to contain costs or to provide financial security. The Committee, in fact, sees several disadvantages:

i) There would be less incentive for Colleges to seek additional income from Conferences or from the recruitment of other students.

ii) The system could result in reductions in the grants made to students by LEA's.

iii) There would be reduced control over the Colleges' range of expenditure.

iv) The system would do nothing to solve the root causes of the current financial problems - over capacity and the small size of some of the institutions.

150. The Advisory Group, as has already been made clear, accepts that over capacity and the size of the institutions needs to be addressed. It also agrees with the ABM Finance Committee that a system of block grants would weaken the Synod's budgetary control over College costs without giving the Principals the financial security they seek. The fixing of a "standard fee" by the Finance Committee, with appearance before the Committee being required only for those Colleges seeking fees above the standard (see Appendix G, Section 6) would similarly weaken control over costs. The Group believes that financial security will come from solving the problems of over capacity and size, rather than from amending the methods of paying fees.

5) A Short-Term Financial Safety Net

151. Nevertheless the Advisory Group recognises that some form of safety net should be provided to cover the short-term problems caused by a deficit of students in a particular year. In our view this should take the form of a guaranteed minimum level of income. The Group recommends that the

ABM Finance Committee's existing system of fee applications and cost analysis should continue on an annual basis, but that the ABM Finance Committee should develop a formula which would give a guarantee that, faced with a substantial fall in the number of both sponsored and total students, a College would receive from the training budget income of, say, 90% of the fee income received from ABM in the previous year, after taking account of inflation. If such a special payment needed to be made, it should be financed by a grant from the training budget as a supplement to the normal fee income for the year. We shall return later to the need to monitor the effectiveness of this measure (see paragraph 225). If this measure is put in place quickly, then there would be no need for a continuation of a financial undertaking to the Theological Colleges once the existing one has come to an end in 1994.

6) Student Numbers and the Capacity of the Colleges

152. At Appendix O, full details are given of the number of sponsored and other students in Theological Colleges over the past 10 years. Appendix P shows equivalent figures for the Methodist and United Reformed Churches.

153. Here we compare the average occupancy of each College over the past 3 years with the information given in the Questionnaire answers as to the potential capacity of each college:

College	Student Numbers (Average for 1989, 1990 & 1991)			Potential Capacity	Notes
	Sponsored	Other*	Total		
Chichester	37	8	45	100	(1)
Cranmer Hall	63	14	77	85	(2)
Lincoln	52	9	61	100	(3)
Mirfield	29	1	30	38	
Oak Hill	58	38	96	96	
Queen's	27	56	83	90	
Ridley Hall	48	5	53	70	
Ripon, Cuddesdon	68	3	71	90	(4)
St John's, Nottm	87	29	116	120	
St Stephen's House	48	10	58	64	
Salisbury and Wells	57	5	62	100	(5)
Trinity	77	62	139	140	
Westcott House	45	9	54	53	
Wycliffe Hall	65	16	81	90	
	761	265	1026	1236	

Notes:
(1) 55 living in the College, the others living out.
(2) Not counting 15 degree students.
(3) Subject to refurbishing the dining room; inexpensive accommodation is available in Lincoln.
(4) This includes students in E.Oxford and Sheffield.
(5) 87 living in the College, the others living out.

154. Although the absolute capacity of the existing Colleges is about 475 students more than the current population of sponsored students, this must be reduced by the number of Methodist, URC and other students that some Colleges and particularly Oak Hill, Queen's, St John's, Nottingham and Trinity, would wish to accommodate to preserve the balance of their institutions. This suggests that the realistic capacity of the Colleges for Church of England ordination candidates is at least 200 above the current numbers and illustrates the conclusion reached on financial grounds in paragraph 145.

* *In many cases "other" refers to students undertaking lay education, but in other cases this includes ordination candidates of other Churches (eg. Cranmer, Lincoln, Queen's). (See Appendix O which gives detailed figures.)*

7) *The Need for a Bishops' Allocation*

155. As mentioned in the note to paragraph 79, the Bishops' Allocation sets a ceiling on the number of sponsored students that may be recruited by each Theological College and is intended to give some protection to the weaker Colleges when there is a dearth of candidates. The effectiveness of such a regulatory mechanism cannot be proved, but it is reasonable to suppose that it has resulted in recent years in some re-routing of candidates from "popular" Colleges to those that were having difficulty in attracting students. The danger of such an arrangement is that, in any extended period of low numbers, it can spread financial problems to more Colleges than might otherwise have been affected. It therefore needs to be implemented with some care. Provided that this is appreciated, however, the Advisory Group believes that the system of Bishops' Allocations is valuable in mitigating the worst effect of "market forces" on the weaker Colleges. In our proposals for the future, we therefore envisage a continuation of the system and suggest the levels at which it should be set and how it should be controlled (see paragraphs 199 and 225).

e) Criteria for Theological Colleges

156. It has been apparent to the Advisory Group from the outset that the current and future needs of the Church of England for ordination training might not require the present complement of 14 Theological Colleges and we have described above why the numbers should, in fact, be reduced (see paragraphs 145 and 154). Anyone who approaches the task of reviewing the provision for theological training would need to guard against being unduly influenced by their own experience of such theological training, some time in the past, and/or by their more recent impressions of the quality of the newly ordained.

157. The Advisory Group therefore thought it essential to establish criteria to define what the Church needs from its future Theological Colleges. Such criteria should enable the existing institutions to be assessed impartially on their current performance and future potential.

158. In developing the criteria, we have distinguished between those which we regard as "essential" to the educational and financial health of an institution training ordinands full-time for the Church's ministry and those which are "desirable". The latter are elements which will assist significantly in the furtherance of our overall strategy for the future, but which are not critical to the survival of a particular institution in the short-term.

159. Against this background, we put forward the following criteria for the assessment of Theological Colleges:

(i) **ESSENTIAL**

Educational

1. Adequate number of ordination candidates from the sponsoring Churches:

   a) to allow viable courses for 3-year degrees, 3-year certificates and 2-year certificates/diplomas
   b) to establish an ethos of ordination training in satisfactory balance with any other kind of training that might be provided by the College

2. Adequate number of staff

   a) to formulate the syllabus/curriculum

   b) to teach the range of subjects (ie. a staff member in each of the main disciplines)
   [Failing this, some credit under this criterion could be given for well-qualified part-time staff able to teach in ways consistent with the College's aims and objectives.]
   c) to provide a variety of viewpoints and illustrate team work
   d) to provide a sufficient body of colleagues for theological and educational debate

3. Reasonable evidence of being able to maintain a satisfactory response to 1 and 2 in the foreseeable future.

4. Adequate response to ACCM Paper No.22:

eg. a) Contemporary methodology in adult education
   b) Integrative approaches
   c) Collaborative styles of ministry

5. Effective provision of pastoral care, spiritual development and ministerial formation.

6. Adequate response to the Bishops' Guidelines for Colleges training women:

a) Staffing
b) Student Numbers
c) Educational Programmes
d) Potential Theological Teachers

7. Resources in the locality for theological education:

a) Theological Courses
b) Appropriate University Departments
c) Colleges of other Churches
d) Church Colleges of Higher Education

8. Full benefit being derived from the available resources:

eg. a) validation for Certificate, Diploma or Degree which is appropriate to the needs of the Church
b) university teaching for appropriate courses
c) provision for postgraduate study for potential theological teachers
d) interaction with university staff
e) interaction with Theological Colleges of other Churches
f) associate or part-time members of staff
g) library facilities
h) staff development

9. Opportunity for the staff to engage in staff development appropriate to the aims and objectives of the College.

Financial

10. Sufficient financial resources to be able to sustain its work, given no upturn in student numbers and at an acceptable fee level (ie. no net current liabilities that cannot be covered without recourse to major loans).

11. Sufficient working capital for foreseeable needs.

12. Adequate premises (both for academic purposes and for staff, and single and married student accommodation) not requiring major repair or modernisation.

13. Demonstrable ability to compensate for shortfalls in numbers of ordination candidates [by recruitment of other students (ie. ordinands

from other Provinces and private students), conference income, lodgers, provision of training services to the region, etc.]

Management

13. A broadly-based and active Governing Body interacting well with a capable Principal and a capable Bursar.

(ii) DESIRABLE

14. Provision of theological education for those who are not full-time students of the College (in satisfactory balance with the training of ordination candidates). This covers, for example, extension studies.

15. Involvement of the College, or its individual staff members, in regional or national activities, including the following:

    a) Theological Courses
    b) Reader training
    c) Lay training
    d) Theological Colleges of other Churches
    e) CME of local dioceses
    f) Youth or other programmes
    g) National Church Agencies
    h) Inter-Anglican and international/ecumenical initiatives in theological education

16. Current use of College premises and library as a resource by the locality or region, by national or international Church organisations.

f) Assessment of Colleges against the Criteria

160. The Advisory Group has carefully assessed each of the Theological Colleges against these Criteria. In doing so, we have drawn on the educational and financial information held by the ABM, amplified by the Principals' responses to the Questionnaire and by the discussions with the representatives of each College and of the ABM Finance Committee (see paragraph 85 to 89). We believe that the judgements we have come to reflect the views of the Bishops' Inspectors and of the relevant ABM Committees. During the course of this overall assessment several important issues emerged. We refer to these below in paragraphs 161 to 166.

161. The Advisory Group was concerned at the wide variation in strengths of staffing between the Colleges (ranging from Mirfield at one end of the spectrum with only four full-time teaching staff to St John's, Nottingham at the other with twelve). It was also concerned at the resulting variations in the opportunities for the interchange of ideas between staff and for staff development.

162. The Group formed the view that the ACCM 22 procedure has provided an effective mechanism to enable Colleges to review their aims and educational programmes and that this has in the majority of cases led to an enhancement of the quality of training provided. Nevertheless, some Colleges (notably Oak Hill and Ridley Hall) have not fully harnessed the opportunities which this procedure provides in terms of contemporary methodology and integrative approaches to theological training.

163. Of the Colleges which train women candidates, more than half do not adequately meet the House of Bishops' Guidelines. Mirfield does not train women for the ordained ministry, nor does its structure as a College provide a model of collaborative ministry.

164. Some Colleges, whether because of their size or location, are not well equipped to handle candidates who are already theology graduates when they enter on their training. Similarly, such Colleges are not able to play their part in producing the theological educators of the future. In fact, there is a two-track system, with the majority of Colleges able to cater for theology graduates and other graduates with high academic achievement or potential and with some confining their educational programmes, whether through inclination or force of circumstances, to the basic requirements of ministerial training and formation. Oak Hill, Chichester and Salisbury and Wells fall into this category. We were told that, as a matter of principle, Mirfield does not consider it an appropriate part of ministerial formation for ordinands at the College to take postgraduate degrees in theology.

165. Not only does this point to the value of Colleges of the size of Trinity, Bristol and St John's, Nottingham where the number of students justifies the recruitment of a strong broadly based teaching faculty, but it also underlines the importance of the University Theology departments which are also available to Colleges in Birmingham, Cambridge, Durham and Oxford, as well as in Bristol, London, Manchester and Nottingham. The existence of local educational resources does not, of course, guarantee that a Theological College will set out to derive benefit from them. It is disappointing, for example, that Oak Hill does not derive more benefit from the teaching resources for theological education available in London.

166. Reduced student numbers have cut into the financial base of certain Colleges. In particular, Chichester, Lincoln, Salisbury and Wells and Westcott House have suffered. Over the years Oak Hill has been generously subsidised by the Kingham Hill Trustees, but even so its fees have been comparable with those at other Colleges. Mirfield has only been able to continue because of the financial and other resources of the Community of the Resurrection. In some of these cases, the low student numbers have led to a weakening of the staff team, in terms of overall size and the range of expertise in different subject areas. Where these Colleges are still strong educationally, the Advisory Group intends to suggest how their share of the available students might be increased. Where, however, Colleges are not only short of students but also educationally weak, the Advisory Group believes that they should no longer be recognised by the House of Bishops. This reduction in the overall number of approved Theological Colleges would create the opportunity to bolster student numbers in those Colleges of greater educational calibre and potential.

g) Conclusions and Proposed Changes

1) Flexibility and Balance

167. In paragraph 145 we stated that, for financial reasons the Advisory Group had reached the inescapable conclusion that the number of Theological Colleges needs to be reduced. The difficult but crucial question is, by how much? Recent numbers of sponsored candidates suggest that in the foreseeable future a capacity to train some 760 ordinands in Theological Colleges will be required. What is almost impossible to predict is the longer term trend. Prudence suggests that the College system should be able to accommodate a future increase of up to 100 above that level (see paragraph 154) and that it should also be able to deal with any contraction that might be required. We have also been aware of the need to provide for a balance among the continuing Colleges to reflect the present spread of church traditions among candidates and this has prompted us to adopt an even-handed policy in the changes we are proposing (see paragraph 200). In reaching conclusions following its assessment of the Theological Colleges, the Advisory Group has therefore borne both these factors in mind.

2) Other Factors

168. The Advisory Group has also taken into account:

i) the minimum size desirable for Colleges (see paragraph 99);

ii) the other educational factors which have been explored earlier in this Report, in particular the desirability of institutions training women and men alongside each other in an integrated manner, the value of close association with the Universities and the need to foster potential theological educators (see paragraphs 100 to 114);

iii) the importance of the Theological Colleges as an educational resource to their local Dioceses (see paragraphs 124 and 125);

iv) the desirability of a geographical spread of Colleges across the country.

3) Assessment

169. The Advisory Group rated each of the Colleges against each of the criteria set out in paragraph 159. Recognising that all the criteria were not of equal value, the Group produced three ranking lists: the first took into account the ratings for all the criteria, the second omitted those for the criteria that were "desirable" rather than "essential" and the third omitted also those for the financial criteria. In each list, the same seven Colleges filled the top seven places, but not always in the same sequence. In alphabetical order, these Colleges were: Cranmer, Queen's, Ripon College, Cuddesdon, St John's Nottingham, Trinity, Westcott and Wycliffe. The Advisory Group concluded that there should be no question of recommending the House of Bishops to withdraw recognition from any of these Colleges, although in each case the Group will be making recommendations as to aspects of the College's future development (see paragraphs 204-213).

170. The seven Colleges in the lower half of the ranking lists were then re-considered with particular reference to the factors highlighted in paragraphs 167 and 168 above.

4) Chichester

171. Chichester Theological College has had four lean years for the recruitment of sponsored ordination candidates and is in a weak position financially. With current student numbers it would be difficult to maintain a balanced teaching staff able to cover the full range of subjects. Nevertheless, the Advisory Group believes that the College has the potential for development.

172. The College's strength is in the area of pastoral care, spiritual development and ministerial formation and it has modern and suitable premises, with scope for growth. The recent ACCM 22 submission has addressed questions of teaching methods and of the supervision and assessment of placements. The new degree and diploma of the School of Theology of the University of Southampton and co-operation with WSIHE and La Sainte Union College clearly offer growth points. The College staff have been actively involved with the surrounding Dioceses in relation both to post-ordination training and CME and to lay training.

173. Provided that the number of sponsored ordination candidates at Chichester can be raised to about 60, the Advisory Group believes that the College can, with its Catholic tradition, play an important role in the training of both male and female ordination candidates and as a theological resource to its surrounding Region.

5) Lincoln

174. Lincoln Theological College has suffered from a reduced intake of sponsored Anglican ordinands over the past six years, but the effect of this has been mitigated by the use of the College since 1987 by the Methodist Church for an increasing number of its ministerial candidates. Nevertheless the College has been running below its economic capacity. This has coincided with work to upgrade the buildings which is now complete, but has caused additional financial strain.

175. The Advisory Group can, however, affirm the quality of the ordination training being offered and the educational developments made in response to ACCM 22, especially for those who are already graduates in theology on entry to training. The College, like St John's, Nottingham, is linked to the University of Nottingham. The Advisory Group believes that closer and developing liaison with St John's, Nottingham would be beneficial to the staff and students of both Colleges. The College is well placed in relation to the north of England but needs to develop a more consistent and committed approach to serving the needs of its Region; its links with the Lincoln LNSM Scheme are useful in this respect.

176. The overall conclusion of the Advisory Group is that the College is a valuable educational resource which should be preserved to the Church, but that for a secure future it needs to attract regularly a minimum of 70 full-time students.

6) Mirfield

177. In its consideration of the College of the Resurrection, Mirfield, the Advisory Group found that the only criteria that were met adequately by the College were the one concerned with pastoral care, spiritual development and ministerial formation and those relating to financial resources. The Group was seriously concerned at the small size of the student body (it gives its potential capacity as 38 and had only 28 ordinands in 1991/92) and at the size and limited range of expertise of the staff team.

178. In an era when men and women serve side by side as ordained clergy and there is increasing collaboration in ministry with the laity, it is unfortunate that the College limits its intake to men and does not offer a model of collaborative ministry. Its response to ACCM 22 has been disappointing: the educational programme and forms of assessment rely heavily on individual written work and there is insufficient opportunity for corporate learning, for communicating understanding and for integration between theology and practice. The College follows the principle that ordinands should not take higher degrees during ordination training; it thus makes no contribution to the development of potential theological teachers.

179. We recognise that Mirfield has a long and honourable tradition of preparing men for the priesthood and that the Community generously serves the Church. Nevertheless the Advisory Group has reached the reluctant but firm conclusion that it must recommend the House of Bishops to withdraw recognition from the College of the Resurrection for ordination training. The Group hopes that the Community of the Resurrection might feel able to make available some of its funds and perhaps even staff to Chichester Theological College, for example by creating a Mirfield lecturer in the area of liturgy or spirituality. We believe that, in the future, there will also be other creative ways in which the Community will be able to serve the Church of England in the training of its ministry.

7) Oak Hill

180. Oak Hill College is the most expensive Theological College in total cost terms. It is situated in an expensive location, the site covers 60 acres and the listed building is costly to run. The College is dependent on the generosity of the Kingham Hill Trust to contain its fees at a level comparable with a number of other Theological Colleges. It has recently been operating at a loss of some £50,000 p.a.

181. The College has a strong tradition of commitment to evangelical theology and an admirable record of offering training to less academically able ordination candidates. It is the only residential Anglican Theological College in the Greater London area and also trains a high number of non-sponsored students.

182. Oak Hill College is however too constrained by its circumstances and, in particular, by its Trust Deed with which the staff are expected to comply. This undoubtedly has restrictive effects on the educational programme and means that it does not benefit satisfactorily from the considerable local resources of theological education. For example, no one may give religious teaching unless prepared to sign a declaration that "he is a Protestant and Evangelical in the strictest sense of the terms".

183. The Advisory Group is concerned at the resulting educational limitations of Oak Hill College. Despite being pressed by ABM under the ACCM 22 procedure, the College's educational programme still does not provide sufficient opportunities for contemporary methodology or integrative approaches to training and the links between practice and theology (especially as regards placements) have not been satisfactorily developed. The College has derived little benefit from the rich teaching resources available in the London area and it has chosen to link for validation purposes with the new Middlesex University, which has no Theology Department. This means that the College would not derive the full educational benefits that accrue to those Colleges which interact with University Departments of Theology. For example, the College would not be open to the same kind of critique or variety of influences as would be the case if it were linked to a university with established theological teaching.

184. The Advisory Group is concerned at the College's inadequate response to the training requirements for women set out in the House of Bishops' Guidelines. The College has attracted only a low proportion of women ordinands. There is no evidence that women's perspectives in theology are appreciated and the woman part-time staff member is used as a tutor for women only.

185. The Advisory Group concludes that, in the light of the various constraints under which it operates, Oak Hill College is not likely to make the changes that are necessary if it is to continue to prepare candidates for ministry in the Church of England. It therefore recommends that the House of Bishops should withdraw recognition from the College for the training of ordinands. The Advisory Group makes this recommendation in the belief that arrangements for a new Regional Course in the area do not depend

on the future of the College (see paragraphs 42 to 52)which might well lie in the field of lay and higher education. If the Kingham Hill Trustees wish to continue their generous contribution to ordination training, the Advisory Group hopes that they might consider offering financial assistance to specific ordinands in consultation with the ABM Grants Secretary.

8) Ridley Hall

186. The Advisory Group recognises the contribution of Ridley Hall and its participation in the ecumenically-shared training of the Cambridge Federation of Theological Colleges. Nevertheless the Group has been seriously concerned at certain aspects of the College's operation and was hesitant about its future.

187. The College's response to ACCM 22 showed a need for further development of its educational programme, particularly with regard to integrative approaches to training and to provision for those entering training who were already graduates in theology. The College has a low number of students including a low proportion of women ordinands and could attend more fully to the particular training needs of the latter. The financial base of the College is weak (as its working capital position indicates) and the premises require further modernisation.

188. Nevertheless, despite these concerns, the Advisory Group recommends that Ridley Hall should continue to be recognised by the House of Bishops. We shall, however, return later in this Report to the question of the future development of the Cambridge Federation (see paragraph 206).

9) St Stephen's House

189. The Advisory Group's main concern about St Stephen's House, springs from the fact that, in recent years, it has been able to recruit only to a level well below its Bishops' Allocation of sponsored candidates and has incurred significant financial losses. It is also in a weak position as regards working capital.

190. Nevertheless the College is well placed in Oxford and meets most of the educational criteria set out in paragraph 159. It has, however, only a low proportion of women students.

191. The Advisory Group believes that, overall, its proposals would result in an increased number of candidates seeking to train at St Stephen's House and that this should bring the required improvement to the College's financial position. It, therefore, recommends that St Stephen's House should

continue to be recognised by the House of Bishops although, later in this Report, it will be commenting on the need for closer association between the Theological Colleges in and near Oxford (see paragraph 207).

10) Salisbury and Wells

192. Salisbury and Wells Theological College has suffered a severe reduction in student numbers, from a high point of 82 (78 sponsored) in 1985/86 down to 58 (51 sponsored) in 1991/92. Furthermore the student entry in 1991/92 was almost exclusively over thirty year-old candidates undertaking a two-year course. The College is not attracting three-year degree candidates or those who are already graduates in theology on entry to training. This suggests that the student body is becoming seriously unbalanced in its composition. The decline in student numbers has forced a reduction in staff and this is the more serious because it cannot easily draw on the teaching resources of the other members of the School of Theology of Southampton University.

193. The College's financial position is insecure. Major repairs and refurbishment will shortly be needed to the premises and, although financial provision has been made for this, shortage of working capital leaves the College in a poor financial position.

194. In view of the uncertainties about recruitment and finance and the lack of educational back-up from a strong University Department of Theology and the lack of other local teaching resources, the Advisory Group recommends that the House of Bishops should withdraw recognition from the College for the training of ordinands. The Group hopes that the Salisbury and Wells Trustees might be prepared to use their residual funds to assist the provision of accommodation in Manchester (see paragraph 198) and finance the trust fund for training laity or serving clergy who are potential theological educators (proposed in paragraph 114).

11) An Ecumenical Development in Manchester

195. Despite these recommendations that recognition should be withdrawn from three existing Theological Colleges, the Advisory Group believes that there is an opportunity for the Church to undertake an innovative venture which could:

- provide "residential" ordination training in an urban setting in the north-west of England

- be established within an ecumenical context

- take advantage of the strong theology faculty in Manchester University (which is as yet unused in conjunction with full-time Anglican theological training)

- open up opportunities for mixed-mode training

- require little capital investment (and possibly none from the Church's own finances).

196. This proposal builds on the fact that NOC is a member of the Northern Federation for Training in Ministry and has its administrative base in Luther King House in Manchester. The Federation's members, in addition to NOC, are the Northern Baptist College, which owns and is situated in Luther King House, and the Methodist Hartley Victoria College and URC Northern College, which are tenants in the building. It currently acts as a hall of residence for about 50 students from the three Colleges, but has a capacity for 70.

197. It is, the Advisory Group believes, a weakness in the Church of England's arrangements for full-time ordination training that, although Westcott House has an Urban Studies Centre in Manchester, there is no residential College in the north-west. More significantly for the future, the Queen's College, Birmingham is the only College that is ecumenical in its constitution. In this connection, the spare capacity at Luther King House is, the Advisory Group believes, an opportunity worth pursuing. No Anglican Theological College has been willing to re-locate to the north-west but, because of the presence of ministerial students from other Churches in Luther King House, it would be practicable to establish a nucleus of full-time Anglican ordination candidates there with relatively low numbers of both students and staff. The proximity of Manchester University, which has one of the strongest theology faculties in the country, would be an added strength and the involvement of NOC could open up opportunities for mixed-mode training.

198. The Advisory Group accordingly recommends that ABM should explore, in conjunction with the Principal of NOC, the Northern Federation, and local Dioceses and educational institutions, the possibility of establishing a nucleus of about 30 Anglican ordinands to be based on Luther King House, in association with NOC, for full-time theological training as part of an integrated institution with the other Churches. Those who could not be accommodated in Luther King House would need to live out. The Advisory Group hopes that the Trustees of Salisbury and Wells Theological College might agree to make funds available to finance the necessary additional staff and student accommodation in the Manchester area. The

stimulation of this ecumenical development will be an important task for the proposed monitoring group (see paragraph 225).

12) The new Bishops' Allocation and its Implications

199. We referred in paragraph 167 to the need to provide some 760 places in Theological Colleges for sponsored candidates and to preserve a balance of church traditions. This can be achieved by increasing the Bishops' Allocation at certain of the continuing institutions and also making provision for an Allocation to Manchester.

College	**Bishops' Allocation 1992/93**	**Sponsored Student Nos. 1991/92**	**Proposed Ceiling for Sponsored Students*** **
Chichester	47	38	60
Cranmer Hall	70	58	77
Lincoln	63	53	70
Mirfield	36	30	-
Oak Hill	66	55	-
Queen's	36	30	37
Ridley Hall	50	45	53
Ripon, Cuddesdon	70	73	74
St John's Nottm	93	89	100
St Stephen's House	56	46	60
Salisbury & Wells	66	51	-
Trinity	79	78	92
Westcott House	46	48	50
Wycliffe Hall	67	63	72
	845	757*	745
Manchester			30***
			775**

* *also 5 students at Edinburgh/Llandaff*

** *In addition, there will continue to be some sponsored candidates training at Coates Hall, Edinburgh and St Michael's, Llandaff or having particular needs met at St Deiniol's Library, Hawarden.*

*** *This assumes the establishment of the Manchester centre. If this is not achieved, the 30 places would need to be re-allocated.*

200. The effect on the balance of church traditions would be:

	1992/93 Bishops' Allocation	Actual Sponsored Students 1991/92	Proposed Ceiling for Sponsored Students
Catholic	139	114	120
Central/Liberal	281	255	261 (including Manchester)
Evangelical	425	388	394
	845	757	775

201. The geographical implications of these proposals are compatible with the Steering Group's proposals for new Regional Courses. In the north, the loss of the College of the Resurrection at Mirfield would be balanced by an Anglican element in the Northern Federation's full-time ministerial training at Luther King House, Manchester. Cranmer Hall would continue as a resource to the Cumbria and North-East Region. In the south, the loss of Salisbury and Wells would make it necessary for SDMTS to find a new base, but various alternatives are available, including Chichester, King Alfred's College, Winchester and WSIHE. The loss of Oak Hill as a Theological College, although it might continue to operate as a lay education centre, would leave Cambridge, Oxford and Chichester as the nearest centres of full-time ordination training to London and the South-East. The Steering Group has already made clear (see paragraph 43) that this area is however rich in other theological resources.

h) Implications of Proposed Changes

1) For Staff and Students

202. The Advisory Group is concerned that the effect on staff and students of any withdrawal of recognition from a Theological College should be mitigated as far as possible. The responsibility for staff welfare lies with the Governing Body, but the Group recommends that the monitoring group proposed in paragraph 225 should liaise closely on this with the Governing Bodies concerned and draw on known counselling facilities for staff members. So far as students are concerned, there would be a particular problem for those currently starting 3 year courses at the affected Colleges. If the House of Bishops decides to withdraw recognition from some Colleges, the effective date would probably be the end of July 1994. College Principals were informed in April 1992 that the undertaking to

students entering College in 1992 that they would be able to complete their training at the same College would apply only to those starting 2 year courses; they were warned that some 3 year students might need to be re-deployed for their third year. Although only a small number might be affected in this way*, it is most important that any disruption to their training or personal circumstances should be kept to the minimum. This would require particular attention by the RSC in consultation with the Colleges and should also be given close oversight by the monitoring group.

2) Financial

203. The Advisory Group has made a thorough analysis of the likely financial effect of the proposals set out above. If no changes were made to the number or structure of Theological Colleges, it would be necessary (unless there was an immediate and significant increase in the total number of sponsored students) for the ABM Finance Committee to increase fees substantially for a number of Colleges to put them on a sound financial footing. Losses of the order experienced recently simply could not continue. The prospect therefore, unless changes are made, is for a significant increase in the cost of training sponsored students at Theological Colleges. On the basis of the proposals in this Report, the Advisory Group calculates that the cost to the Church of training students in the new structure, as well as enabling the Colleges to make reasonable provision for major repairs, is likely to be similar (given the same number of students and ignoring inflation) to the cost of training students at present. The Advisory Group believes that the proposals would save the Church from an otherwise inevitable escalation in fees and enable the continuing Colleges to operate on a better financial basis, though this does not solve the problem of the provision of capital for certain of the Colleges.

i) Future Development of the Continuing Theological Colleges

204. The proposals in this Report allow for 11 of the 14 Theological Colleges to continue to train ordination candidates for the Church of England and recommend the establishment of a new unit within the Northern Federation in Manchester. The longer term future of some of these Colleges will depend on whether the flow of sponsored candidates to the Theological Colleges is maintained at or above the current level. Should the flow decrease the Advisory Group believes that it should be the duty of the monitoring group which is proposed later in this Report (see

* *At the 3 affected Colleges a total of 10 3-year sponsored students entered training in 1991. The figure for 1992 is not yet available.*

paragraph 225) to bring the implications to the attention of the House of Bishops. It also believes that its proposals would accommodate any further necessary contraction without severe disruption to the overall framework.

205. In its assessment of the 11 continuing Theological Colleges, the Advisory Group reached the conclusion, in the light of all the evidence before it, that, in all cases, some development was needed to match the College's structure and educational programmes to the requirements of the Church for the training of ordinands into the twenty-first century. These desirable developments are set out below. The Advisory Group recommends that progress by the Colleges in these areas should be supervised by the monitoring group.

1) The Cambridge Colleges

206. The Advisory Group recommends that Ridley Hall and Westcott House should continue to address seriously, in consultation with the other Colleges in the Cambridge Federation and with the General Synod's Council for Christian Unity, how to develop the Cambridge Federation as an ecumenical body in a way which takes account of the current ecumenical situation in Britain and the specific training requirements of each Church. This could lead to a further rationalisation of College sites and to the formation of units of the size envisaged in paragraph 99 above.

2) The Oxford Colleges

207. The Advisory Group looked very carefully at the heavy concentration of residential places in Oxford and the problems thereby created for the whole system of full-time theological training. However, it came to the conclusion that it would be inopportune at the present time to impede the changes that are currently in hand. The discussions between Ripon College, Cuddesdon, St Stephen's House and Wycliffe Hall, together with the Oxford Ministry Training Course are a valuable initiative and their impetus should be maintained. These institutions see themselves in a process of mutual development and have a common supervisory committee for their educational programmes and assessment. The Advisory Group recommends that consideration should continue to be given to joint appointments and to the formation of an appropriate structural arrangement so that continued collaboration does not depend solely on the initiative of the current Principals and staffs. It is encouraging that the Oxford Certificate is becoming a B.Th degree of the University. The three Colleges should make the maximum use of the opportunities afforded by their University context, including particularly the opportunities for those who enter training as graduates in theology and for those who are potential

theological teachers. Consideration should also be given to involving the Colleges of other Churches, especially Mansfield, Regents Park and Westminster, in the further development of ecumenical theological education in Oxford.

3) Chichester Theological College

The challenge for Chichester Theological College is to work collaboratively with other institutions so as to broaden the appeal of the training it offers while remaining an explicitly Catholic College. It should also explore vigorously what support it can provide to the SDMTS in terms of teaching, library and administrative resources and accommodation.

4) Cranmer Hall, Durham

The Advisory Group is aware of the contribution which Cranmer Hall is making especially to the northern Dioceses. The Group also welcomes the College's growing links with the Roman Catholic seminary at Ushaw and with the Wesley Study Centre in Durham. It is recommended that these developments should be pursued and that the College should more actively seek to be a resource to part-time ordination training in the Cumbria and North-East Region.

5) Lincoln Theological College

As mentioned already in paragraph 175, the Advisory Group considers that Lincoln Theological College should draw closer to St John's, Nottingham, in terms of student contact and staff liaison and development. It also needs to become more committed to serving the needs of its Region and, in particular, should explore what further resource it can provide as a support to part-time ordination training.

6) The Queen's College, Birmingham

The Advisory Group recognises the pioneering ecumenical work achieved by the Queen's College. The College should now, however, take stock of its progress in the light of the current ecumenical situation in Britain. It should consider, in consultation with the General Synod's Council for Christian Unity, the Division of Ministries of the Methodist Church and the Ministerial Training Committee of the URC, whether the ecumenism which it is consciously developing is too far ahead of the current ecumenical situation and whether it is therefore an effective preparation for ordinands to deal with the circumstances of the Church as they exist. The College should also address the question whether there is a sufficient presence of

Anglicans and Methodists amongst the balance of staff appointments to be able to handle adequately the specific training requirements of the two Churches and, not least, to meet the Bishops' Guidelines for Colleges and Courses Training Women. Finally, the College should consider whether its black studies course is sufficiently integrated into the content of the overall educational programme of the College.

7) St John's College, Nottingham

212. In paragraph 210 we have stressed the desirability of close liaison between St John's College and Lincoln Theological College. We note that St John's has recently been making more effective use of links with the Department of Theology of the University of Nottingham and hope that these will continue to be developed. We are concerned however that the College should give more attention to the need to train ordinands for the specific requirements of parochial ministry in the Church of England. The closer link with Lincoln, referred to above, could well assist with this.

8) Trinity College, Bristol

213. The Advisory Group notes that Trinity College has achieved degree validation, following the closure of CNAA, with the University of Bristol. In this connection, it will be important for the College to integrate its pastoral studies and its courses in spirituality fully into its educational programme. The Advisory Group recommends that Trinity should also review the effectiveness of its Walsall project and the degree to which that is integrated into the content of the College's educational programme. The Advisory Group is also concerned that the College should develop closer links with the Methodist Church's Wesley College in Bristol.

E. THE PROPOSED WAY AHEAD

a) Links with the Education System, the Dioceses and other Churches

214. In setting out the educational issues which it had identified during its work, the Advisory Group drew attention to a number of areas in which the Theological Colleges could, with benefit, interact either with the education system or with the education and training initiatives of the Dioceses. These apply equally to the part-time Theological Courses.

215. The main areas would appear to be:

i) Deriving maximum benefit from the theological teaching resources available in the University:

strengthening the link between academic theology and ministerial training; encouraging and benefiting from the development of relevant modular degree courses, using university expertise to validate College and Course educational programmes; improving the quality of staff in both the University and theological training systems by cross-fertilisation in teaching (see paragraphs 103 to 109).

ii) *Deriving maximum benefit from collaboration with the CCHE's:*

sharing teaching staff and facilities including libraries; sharing residential facilities and technical services; encouraging the exchange of experience between ordinands and those training for other professions; sharing insights on models of professional formation (see paragraphs 115 to 120).

iii) *Contributing to the vocational, educational and training initiatives of the Dioceses:*

offering specialist support in areas of CME, of lay training including Reader training and of adult education; making available modules of ordination training which could be relevant to the training of LNSM's (see paragraph 124).

216. Earlier in this Report, the Steering Group stressed the importance of mutual collaboration between the Churches in the establishment of the national network of part-time Courses so that use of the structure can be made on an ecumenical basis in every part of the country (see paragraph 22). Similarly, in its assessment of the individual Theological Colleges, the Advisory Group has been impressed by the value being gained by ecumenical links between Colleges. Its proposal for an Anglican residential presence in Luther King House springs as much from this as from geographical considerations (see paragraphs 195 to 198).

b) The Concept of Regional Consortia

217. Both groups believe that the way ahead for theological training lies in strengthening all these links, so that all those in the education system and the Churches contributing to theological training and education are brought closer together. This will strengthen isolated initiatives, improve the quality of training, make the most effective and economic use of resources and offer a much broader canvas for staff development. The process will not

happen by itself - or at least, not with equal effectiveness throughout the country. This has brought us to the view that a Consortium should be set up in each of the 8 Regions identified by the Steering Group, to act as a focus and catalyst for this process.

218. The Theological College Principals stressed in their paper (see Appendix G, Sections 3 and 4) the need for Colleges and Courses to be partners in resource with each other and with other institutions serving their regions, but they acknowledge the difficulties of implementing such a strategy. We see the Regional Consortium as the crucial factor in transforming aspirations into achievement.

219. As long ago as 1975, an ACCM Working Party, in the Report "Alternative Patterns of Training" (GS 265), recommended the establishment of ten Regional Centres to "draw together all forms of training, residential and non-residential, into one comprehensive yet many-sided scheme". These were intended to be strong residential institutions with the character of Theological Colleges, but used for wider purposes. We wish to stress that our own proposal is not based on one central establishment in each Region, but rather on drawing into close partnership the existing institutions for maximum mutual support and to lessen the risk of duplication of effort.

220. The aim of each Regional Consortium would be to facilitate dialogue between the various educational interests so that they could influence and assist each other and also to develop a complementary dialogue between them, on the one hand, and the Dioceses and other Churches on the other. The objective of these dialogues would be to enable training and educational needs to be met through the most economic use of resources by avoiding duplication of effort and developing creative and flexible possibilities for training. To this end, each Regional Consortium should have the following specific tasks:

i) to ensure that the Theological Colleges and Courses in the Region make the optimum use of the resources (eg. academic, library, accommodation) of the Universities, CCHE's, Colleges/Seminaries of other Churches and other institutions of theological education and, in turn, make reciprocal resource contributions;

ii) to ensure that the Theological Colleges and Courses develop their potential as resources to the whole Church, contributing, where appropriate, to clergy in-service training, LNSM training, lay training and adult education in the Dioceses;

iii) to bring the Colleges and Courses together with the local Dioceses and other Churches in creating imaginative opportunities for training and lay education;

iv) to integrate training programmes

   a) to allow orderly progression by students (eg. by use of CATS and assessment of prior learning),

   b) to maximise the use of common modules of training where elements of different training programmes overlap;

v) to encourage the use of flexible methods of training (eg. mixed-mode - a combination of part-time and full-time training);

vi) to coordinate staffing policies (to avoid duplication of appointments and to provide mutual cover);

vii) to foster opportunities for cooperation in staff development;

viii) to bring before ABM and the appropriate authorities in the other Churches any national policy issues which arise from the work of the Consortium.

221. Each Regional Consortium should be chaired by a senior Church leader and have core membership from each Theological College and/or Course in the Region and each Diocese. It should invite the fullest possible participation from representatives of the relevant Regions/Districts of other Churches, University Departments of Theology, CCHE's, Colleges/Seminaries of other Churches and other institutions of theological education.

222. We see this as a process of evolution which could open up the opportunities for radical revisions in the pattern of ordination training in the longer term. It would be possible through the agency of a Regional Consortium to experiment with an entirely new approach to ordination training, whereby an ordinand would be parish-based, with a local tutor to aid reflection on ministerial experience, and carrying out academic study either in blocks of several weeks at a time in a College or through the medium of a part-time Course. Such an approach could bring significant benefits through closer integration of learning, theology and ministry, involve Dioceses and parishes more actively in ordination training and lessen the problems of upheaval for married candidates. Dr Tetley

presented a paper to the Advisory Group outlining this approach in more detail. The paper is attached as Appendix Q.

223. The establishment of Regional Consortia would also have significance if circumstances required any further reduction in the number of Theological Colleges, easing the way to closer federation or union of institutions within a Region.

F. CONCLUSION

224. In this Report we have:

i) described the work that still remains to be done in each Region to establish stable arrangements for part-time ordination training;

ii) recommended a reduction in the number of Theological Colleges and outlined developments required in the continuing Colleges;

iii) suggested how the vital links between Theological Colleges and Courses on the one hand and the education system, the Dioceses and the other Churches on the other can be strengthened by a pattern of Regional Consortia.

225. If the House of Bishops accepts the general direction of these recommendations and wishes them to be implemented, we believe that it will be essential for the House to act quickly and decisively. We recommend that ABM be instructed to set up a monitoring group to manage the transition on behalf of the House and to report to the House, not less than annually, on progress. We see such a group as having the following tasks:

i) To ensure a satisfactory evolution of the new Regional Courses, along the lines set out in this Report (see paragraphs 30 to 71), to supervise the process of their recognition (see paragraph 77) and to refer any problems to the Standing Committee of the House for resolution.

ii) To see that any transitional costs relating to the new structure of Regional Courses (see paragraph 75) are approved in advance by the ABM Finance Committee.

iii) To consider, with the ABM Finance Committee, the results of the "trial run" of the new financial arrangements for the Regional Courses and consult, as necessary, with the Central Board of Finance and the Standing Committee of the House of Bishops on the resolution of any significant problems that arise (see paragraph 76).

iv) To keep under review the educational and financial stability of the new Regional Courses.

v) To liaise with the Governing Bodies of those Colleges from which recognition is withdrawn who will be overseeing the management and welfare of staff (see paragraph 202).

vi) To monitor the cessation of ordination training at those Theological Colleges from which the House of Bishops withdraws recognition, consulting with the Colleges and ABM on such matters as the relocation of 3-year students and any special financial requirements brought about by the transition (see paragraph 202).

vii) To stimulate the development of the Manchester Project in consultation with local Dioceses, the NOC and other Churches (see paragraph 195 to 198).

viii) To monitor changes in the financial position of the continuing Colleges and their development as proposed in paragraphs 206-213 above.

ix) To monitor the flow of students to the Theological Colleges and bring to the attention of the House of Bishops as part of its periodic reports the implications of any significant increase or decrease in the level, overall or at any particular College (see paragraphs 167 and 204)

x) To advise the Bishops' Committee for Ministry annually on the level of Bishops' Allocation appropriate for each College (see paragraph 155).

xi) To assess, after 3 years, the effectiveness of the short-term financial safety net proposed in paragraph 151 and to report on this to the House of Bishops.

xii) To encourage the development of a Consortium in each Region and to report progress to the House of Bishops.

xiii) To collate responses to this Report and to summarise these for the House of Bishops to consider at its meeting in January 1993.

xiv) To report to the House of Bishops, in the light of its monitoring work, on any other measures that may be needed to ensure the appropriate and efficient use of resources for theological training.

226. This monitoring group should be established for a period of not more than 5 years in the first instance. ABM should then give to the House of Bishops a full report of developments and as to the need for further work. We recommend that the group should be chaired by a Diocesan Bishop, appointed by the House of Bishops, who would become a member of the Bishops' Committee for Ministry. Members of the group should be appointed by ABM, on behalf of the House of Bishops, and should be selected so as to enable the concerns of the Bishops' Inspectors, appropriate ABM Committees (especially IMEC, EVSC, RSC and Finance), women in ministry and Theological Colleges and Courses to be fully represented. The group should include representatives of the Methodist and United Reformed Churches and have available to it advice from the Board of Education.

227. In conclusion we wish to reiterate our concern at the fragility of the part-time Theological Courses in many parts of the country and at the financial situation of many of the Theological Colleges. The situation brooks no delay. Whilst urging on the House of Bishops the need for firm and speedy action to deal with the immediate issues raised in our Report, we hope that the House will also grasp the long-term opportunity to forge closer links, at Regional level and in an ecumenical context, between all those parties concerned with theological education and training.

SUMMARY OF RECOMMENDATIONS*

Paragraph Reference

In relation to the work which the Steering Group has been carrying out with the Courses, the House of Bishops is invited to: 77

1) endorse the essential considerations (paragraph 22) and structural characteristics (paragraph 23) developed by the Steering Group;

2) agree the line of approach currently being recommended for each of the 8 Regions (paragraphs 30-71) and to underline the need for the existing Courses to be fully committed to these developments so that quick progress can be made;

3) note that the House will be asked formally to recognise each new Regional Course as soon as -

   a) its submission under the ACCM 22 procedure has been cleared by the EVSC (paragraph 14.i)),

   and

   b) the Advisory Board of Ministry has accepted that the proposals for the Course represent an adequate response to the recommendations of ACCM 30 with regard to educational factors, staffing levels and management structure (paragraph 14.ii)),

   and

   c) the ABM Finance Committee has agreed any special financial arrangements needed to enable the existing Course(s) to move to the new structure (paragraph 75);

4) agree that the ABM Finance Committee and the Courses should be requested to carry out a "trial run" of a new fee application form for 1993/94, on the new arrangement and as if the new structure was in place, in tandem with the normal fee application process for that year (paragraph 76);

* *Note: These recommendations start from the base that the House of Bishops has already endorsed the recommendations of ACCM 30.*

In relation to the work of the Advisory Group, the House of Bishops is invited to:

5) endorse the view that elements of "residence" are indispensable aspects of the theological training provided by both Colleges and Courses; 95

6) agree that 60 full-time students is the absolute minimum size at present for a non-federated Theological College, but that the aim should be for an evolution towards units of 100 to 120 students for all Theological Colleges; 99

7) endorse the view that an institution which does not train women alongside men, in an integrated manner, is not preparing men adequately for the ministry they will be exercising after the ordination; 102

8) agree that a formal shift of responsibility for ordination training to the Universities is neither practicable nor desirable; 103

9) endorse the view that the Church needs access to a range of University courses so as to allow both those with high educational potential and candidates of average attainment to participate in University education; 108

10) agree that every Theological College should be staffed sufficiently strongly to be able to encourage candidates who are potential theological educators and supervise them where appropriate; 113

11) agree that a trust fund should be established to enable grants to be made by the ABM Further Degrees Panel to laity and serving clergy who are potential theological educators; 114

12) endorse the view that it is not practicable at present for ordinands to be trained in Church Colleges of Higher Education or for CCHE's to take over responsibility for providing part of theological training for ordinands; 116

13) encourage Theological Colleges to cooperate with CCHEs to take advantage of the resources available in the latter; 119

14) encourage Theological Colleges and Courses to respond to current modular developments in education; 122

15) ask the Church Commissioners, when a more favourable financial climate obtains, to make equity-sharing loans available once more to Theological Colleges; 128

16) endorse the conclusion that the overall number of Theological Colleges needs to be reduced and that "market forces" should not be allowed to determine the outcome; 145/6

17) agree that the present method of paying fees should continue; 150

18) endorse the current method of agreeing Theological College fees adopted by the ABM Finance Committee; 151

19) invite the ABM Finance Committee to develop a formula which would give a guarantee that, faced with a substantial fall in the number of both sponsored and total students, a Theological College would receive from the training budget income of, say, 90% of the fee income received from ABM in the previous year, after taking account of inflation; 151

20) accept that the present financial undertaking to Theological Colleges should not continue beyond 1994; 151

21) agree that a system of Bishops' Allocations of sponsored ordination candidates to Theological Colleges should be continued (see also 29 below); 155

22) endorse the criteria for the assessment of Theological Colleges set out in paragraph 159; 159

23) encourage Theological Colleges to harness the opportunities which the ACCM 22 procedure provides in terms of contemporary methodology and integrative approaches to theological training; 162

24) agree that the objective should be for Theological Colleges to have at present the capacity to train some 760 ordinands but with flexibility to train a further 100 should that be required or to contract to a lower level; 167

25) endorse the importance of Theological Colleges as an educational resource to their local Dioceses; 168

26) endorse the desirability of a geographical spread of Theological Colleges across the country and also a balance of Church traditions; 167/168

27) agree that recognition for the training of ordination candidates should be withdrawn after July 1994 from the College of the Resurrection, Mirfield, Oak Hill College and Salisbury and Wells Theological College; 179, 185 and 194

28) invite ABM to explore the possibility of establishing a nucleus of about 30 Anglican ordinands in Luther King House, Manchester; 198

29) agree that from September 1994 the Bishops' Allocation of sponsored ordination candidates at the continuing Theological Colleges should be as proposed in paragraph 199; 199

30) endorse the lines of future development for the continuing Theological Colleges set out in paragraphs 206 to 213; 206-213

In relation to the future strategy recommended by both Groups, the House of Bishops is invited to:

31) endorse the emphasis placed by both Groups on the value of ecumenical cooperation in theological training; 216

32) endorse the objective of establishing Regional Consortia throughout the country with the tasks set out in paragraph 220 and the composition given in paragraph 221; 220/221

33) authorise the ABM to establish immediately, under the Chairmanship of a Diocesan Bishop appointed by the House of Bishops, a monitoring group to supervise the implementation of the above recommendations and with the specific tasks set out in paragraph 225; 225

34) agree that the composition of the monitoring group should be as set out in paragraph 226. 226

ADDENDUM

Extracts from:

THEOLOGICAL TRAINING in the Church of England

This booklet is intended primarily for Church of England candidates for the ordained and for the accredited lay ministry. Every effort has been made to ensure its accuracy at the time of going to press.

ADVISORY BOARD OF MINISTRY
Church House, Great Smith Street, London SW1P 3NZ

NOTES ON TRAINING

Ordained and Accredited Lay Ministry

SELECTION

Candidates should be commended in the first place to the Diocesan Director of Ordinands or Diocesan Lay Ministry Adviser. Before being accepted for training they are required under the regulations approved by the Bishops:

1. to have the necessary educational qualifications or show that they have the potential to benefit from formal courses of training (this may involve being asked to undertake a preliminary course of study before being sponsored);

2. to be sponsored by their Bishop for attendance at a Bishops' Selection Conference;

3. to satisfy medical requirements.

Candidates for non-stipendiary ministry should be well established in their community, local church and occupation, and normally should be over the age of 30.

Candidates for local non-stipendiary ministry should be well established in their community, local church and occupation; and their circumstances should, as far as possible, assure that they will remain in their present locality. Candidates should be at least thirty years old. They will normally be under the age of 60 and over the age of 40.

EDUCATIONAL QUALIFICATIONS

Candidates are required to have the following qualifications:

1. **Under 25**. Five passes in academic subjects in GCE, one of which must be English Language, and two at 'A' level, or equivalent qualifications. (Candidates with a recognised professional qualification are normally exempt from all entrance requirements, as

are those who have HNC or HND or BTec National Certificate/Diploma together with an 'O' level or its equivalent in English Language. Other qualifications are taken into consideration, but very little credit is usually given for half-finished professional qualifications; candidates should normally complete these before going forward). The only exceptions to this rule are for candidates who are recommended for entry to the Aston Training Scheme. No academic qualifications are required for this part-time course, but the Bishops' Selectors will need to be assured that candidates for this scheme are capable of participating in the course satisfactorily.

2. **Aged 25 and over.** The academic standard is not laid down in terms of GCE or in any other absolute form, but each individual is considered and assessed in accordance with their existing qualifications and the type of training which they should do, if accepted as a candidate.

TRAINING

1. Pre-theological training

Candidates under 35 may be required to undertake the Aston Training Scheme prior to beginning their theological training. The Aston Training Scheme takes the form of part-time training for two years. On completion of the Aston course to the satisfaction of the Assessors, candidates undertake theological training in compliance with the regulations set out below.

Further details may be obtained from ABM or from The Principal, The Aston Training Scheme, 148 Court Oak Road, Harborne, Birmingham B17 9AB. Tel: 021 427 5225.

The Simon of Cyrene Theological Institute provides a pre-theological course and also gives assistance to Colleges and Courses, dioceses and participating Churches with the initial and in-service training of clergy as well as lay education and theological research with regard to 'black' issues. Further details may be obtained from ABM or from the Principal, The Simon of Cyrene Theological Institute, 2 St Ann's Crescent, Wandsworth, London SW18 2LR. Tel: 081 874 1353.

2. Theological training

Candidates should always consult their Bishop or Diocesan Director of Ordinands or Diocesan Lay Ministry Adviser before applying to a theological College or Course for admission. A recommendation to train for ordination from the Bishops' Selectors does not carry with it the right of acceptance by any particular theological College or Course.

A candidate wishing to undertake a course of training varying from the Regulations approved by the Bishops (including study for a higher degree) should inform the DDO or DLMA in order that the advice of the ABM Recruitment and Selection Committee may be sought.

i) *Candidates under 30*

a) Graduates in theology (where at least half of the degree consists of theology) spend two years on a full-time course at a theological College and have to fulfil the Bishops' requirements by satisfactorily completing a course of education approved on behalf of the House of Bishops by ABM.

b) Graduates in subjects other than theology are required to spend three years on a full-time course at a theological College and have to fulfil the Bishops' requirements by satisfactorily completing a course of education approved on behalf of the House of Bishops by ABM. Only those candidates with an upper second or first class degree may read for a degree in theology or postgraduate diploma in theology, unless the degree course is specially designed as a training course for the professional ministry, is approved by ABM, and involves no additional expense or lengthening of the normal course of training. Certain special courses and professional qualifications may be regarded as conferring graduate status.

c) Non-graduates are required to spend three years on a full-time course at a theological College and to fulfil the Bishops' requirements by satisfactorily completing a course of education approved on behalf of the House of Bishops by ABM.

ii) *Candidates aged 30 - 49*

a) Candidates for stipendiary ministry are required to undertake either two years full-time training at a theological College, or three years part-time training on a theological Course. In some instances the recommendations for training will indicate a preferred form. Candidates are required to fulfil the Bishops' requirements by satisfactorily completing a course of education approved on behalf of the House of Bishops by ABM.

b) Candidates for non-stipendiary ministry are required to undertake three years part-time training on a theological Course, and to fulfil the Bishops' requirements by satisfactorily completing a course of education approved on behalf of the House of Bishops by ABM.

iii) *Candidates aged 50 and over*

a) Candidates for stipendiary ministry usually undertake either two years full-time training at a theological College, or three years part-time training on a theological Course. The exact nature of the training is decided by the sponsoring bishop.

b) Candidates for non-stipendiary ministry usually undertake three years part-time training on a theological Course. The exact nature of the training is decided by the sponsoring bishop.

NB. In each of the above regulations the age refers to the candidate's age at the start of training.

The Bishops' *Regulations for Non-Stipendiary Ministry* can be found in ACCM Occasional Paper No.23, March, 1987, which is available from the ABM, priced 50p.

GRANTS

Candidates who have been recommended for training for ordination are eligible for financial help from Central Church Funds, but should always obtain as much assistance as possible from other sources before applying for such grants. Local Education Authorities almost invariably make awards to candidates who will be undertaking a first degree course during training, but discretionary awards are also available and also awards for the support of dependents.

Married candidates should note that grants from Central Church Funds are not available for the maintenance of dependents; they should always carefully consult with the appropriate diocesan authority, which has the responsibility to ensure adequate funds are available for family support.

Further details about grants may be obtained from the appropriate diocesan authority or from ABM.

UNIVERSITY COURSES IN THEOLOGY

Candidates for ministry wishing to undertake a degree should consult their Director of Ordinands, Diocesan Lay Ministry Adviser, or others with expert knowledge, such as a Headteacher or Careers Adviser, about the choice of University and the courses available both there and at other Institutes and Colleges of Higher Education.

Full details of all relevant courses are given in the *Degree Course Guide, Theology and Religious Studies in UK Universities, Polytechnics and Colleges*, published for the Careers Research and Advisory Council by Hobsons Press (Cambridge) Ltd., Bateman Street, Cambridge, CB2 1LZ, and revised every two years. The latest edition, edited by Dr R Gordon, was published in 1990-91, price £4.75.

As changes are frequent, all information should be checked with the University or College concerned. Five GCE passes, two at 'A' level, are the usual minimum requirements. Applications for places at all Universities for England and Wales must be made by through the Universities Central Council on Admissions, PO Box 28, Cheltenham, Gloucestershire, GL50 1HY.

The Polytechnics Central Admissions System (PCAS) provide a free guide for applicants, available from PCAS, PO Box 67, Cheltenham, Gloucestershire GL50 3SF. Applications for the courses at other Institutions should be made direct to the College concerned.

Those courses or options which give the fullest weight to Scripture, Doctrine and Church History are most likely to qualify for exemptions. Certain University courses and some of the Church Colleges' or HE Colleges' degrees, have been specially designed with ministerial requirements in mind; at other Universities a careful choice of options may give exemptions not only in these subjects but also in Liturgy, Ethics or the Pastoral Studies Introductory Course.

TRAINING IN THE COLLEGES AND COURSES

Professional ministry demands a knowledge of the Christian faith, an understanding of it in relation to human life and an ability to present it effectively in the contemporary world. Training and assessment therefore seek to develop, and to test insofar as is possible, the candidates' grasp of the faith they will be authorised to preach and teach.

Each theological College and Course has prepared an account of the theological training which it offers on behalf of the Church in response to proposals agreed by the House of Bishops in 1986 and published in ACCM Occasional Paper No.22, entitled *Education for the Church's Ministry*. This booklet is available from the ABM priced £1.00. Each College and Course has considered the aims and objectives for training, the educational programme and forms of assessment, in response to the following three questions:

a) What ordained ministry does the Church of England require?
b) What is the shape of the educational programme best suited for equipping people to exercise this ministry?
c) What are the appropriate means of assessing suitability for the exercise of this ministry?

The entries from the Colleges and Courses which follow indicate the overall approach and priorities of each College and Course at the current time.

The national network of part-time theological Courses is currently under discussion, with a Steering Group for Theological Courses acting on behalf of the House of Bishops. The provision which is outlined in this booklet may be subject to change, especially in the period between August, 1992 and 1994. Any new arrangements will ensure that every part of each diocese is covered by a course of part-time theological training which is approved on behalf of the House of Bishops by ABM.

LOCAL NON-STIPENDIARY MINISTRY

Arrangements for training are the responsibility of the sponsoring Bishop, and should be discussed with the Bishop or Diocesan Director of Ordinands or Diocesan Lay Ministry Adviser. The Bishops' Regulations and Guidelines can be found in *Local NSM*, ABM Policy Paper No.1, April, 1991, which is available from ABM priced £1.50.

CHURCH ARMY

Candidates for the Church Army are selected by the Church Army itself. Further details of educational qualifications and selection procedures can be obtained from The Candidates Secretary, Church Army Headquarters, Independents Road, Blackheath, SE3 9LG.

Candidates train for three years at the Wilson Carlile College of Evangelism, and qualify for their ministry as Evangelists by the externally examined Diploma in Evangelism.

READERS

Candidates should be commended in the first place to the Diocesan Warden of Readers by their parish priest. Full information about selection and training as a Reader may be obtained from the appropriate Diocesan Readers' Board Secretary or Warden.

The Report *The Training of Readers*, ACCM Occasional Paper No.32, November, 1989, sets out the overall priorities in the training of Readers in the Church of England, and is available from the ABM priced £1.00. The Bishops' Regulations for Reader Ministry are set out in ABM Policy Paper No.2, June, 1991, available from the ABM priced £1.20.

PRE-THEOLOGICAL TRAINING COURSES

The Aston Training Scheme

The Aston course provides a two-year, part-time foundation programme for the Church's ministry. Access to the Scheme is through a recommendation by a Bishops' Selection Conference, where a candidate is recognised to have potential for ministry but is felt to need an opportunity for further development before proceeding to a theological College or Course.

For some, Aston will provide the guidance to enable them to develop in their personal life, to work through disabling experiences and to gain self-confidence and greater personal integration. For others, the demanding training will test further the strength of their vocation and its effect upon their families, whilst the diversity of Church styles represented in the Aston community will enrich their own spiritual discipline. Others needing to gain a deeper understanding of the nature of society and its systemic ills, as the context for ministry, will benefit from the Social Sciences course option and the method of 'doing theology' that Aston has developed. For some others, Aston will provide the opportunity to acquire study skills and to gain academic self-confidence. What matters most is the integration of all aspects of life: personal, intellectual, social and spiritual; and a proper balance of family, work, leisure and study.

The course that has been designed to meet these needs is a demanding programme of study, reflection and experience. It is a mix of residential events - four weekends and two weeks each year, private study and intensive personal work with a Pastoral Tutor who is assigned to each student. Students are subject to a rigorous assessment process including self-assessment and must satisfy External Assessors in order to proceed to College. However, the greatest resource on which we build is the wealth of skills, experiences and abilities provided by the students themselves. Thus, though all teaching styles are used, self-directed, participatory and experiential adult educational practice is preferred. Aston may be viewed as a fellowship of vocation in which spouses and families are encouraged to participate fully in the Aston community. The Scheme embodies the conviction that a high level of self-awareness, group and personal skills informed by the habits of spiritual discipline and theological exploration, are pre-requisites in ministerial formation.

The Simon of Cyrene Theological Institute

The Simon of Cyrene Theological Institute was opened in Autumn 1989, and there was a ceremony in April 1990 to mark its dedication and formal inauguration. Although a Church of England initiative, it has attracted full ecumenical participation. It is based in South London, through the generosity of the Diocese of Southwark, but has assumed national dimensions. It has rapidly become a significant resource centre for theological education, training and research from the perspective of the black experience. Its responsibilities therefore include a pre-theological Course to assist black candidates; Pastoral Studies Units and Racism Awareness Worshops for white and black students in Colleges and Courses; in-service training for white and black clergy; lay education and theological research. The resources of the Institute are available to the Churches generally and other institutions concerned for the empowerment of black people. For instance, it is expected that a BA Access Course in Theology and Religious Studies and Social Administration will be initiated at the Institute in September, 1992, in collaboration with the Roehampton Institute through which accreditation will be granted by the University of Surrey.

The aims and objectives of the pre-theological Course which can be taken on a part-time as well as full-time basis, are as follows:

1. To develop a critical awareness of the world and the Church's mission in it.

2. To help students discover their identity and to gain in self-confidence.

3. To promote learning skills, and skills in the practice of theology.

4. To promote leadership skills and an understanding of community dynamics.

5. To assist in the growth of awareness and pride among the black leadership and ministers of the Church.

Parochial placements are an integral part of the programme.

In addition to the Principal, there is a full-time Overseas Research Fellow and two part-time Lecturers as well as various tutors. The staff is ecumenical in composition.

FULL-TIME COURSES AT THEOLOGICAL COLLEGES

Chichester Theological College

Chichester is the oldest of the present Anglican Colleges, founded in 1839 during the early phase of the Oxford Movement. This catholic heritage informs the life and worship of the College. Our students - men and women, married and unmarried - come from a wide variety of backgrounds. The College seeks to provide them with a firm discipline of prayer and worship, a sound theological education, and a thorough introduction to pastoral life and ministry, to enable them to become faithful, positive and critical ministers of word and sacrament.

The College occupies purpose-built buildings, the larger part of which were opened in 1987. It enjoys close links with Chichester Cathedral, two seminaries in Bavaria, and the Anglican Institute in St Louis, Missouri, whose Director, Bishop Michael Marshall, teaches in the College. His participation underlines the College's commitment to the formation of an evangelistic ministry for today's Church, in the best Tractarian tradition.

The College is a constituent part of the University of Southampton School of Theology and Religion. The College trains some men and women for the non-stipendiary ministry, some men for the permanent diaconate, and admits full-time and part-time non-ministerial students. A significant number of students are from overseas.

All students who complete the course satisfactorily are awarded the Chichester Certificate in Ministerial Theology. This includes the study of the bible, doctrine and liturgy, church history, ethics, ministry and mission; and also pastoral fieldwork in the form of weekly local attachments, and an annual placement. The Certificate is awarded to both two and three-year candidates, but for three-year students the course can additionally lead to the award of the Southampton Degree of Bachelor of Theology, either at Honours or ordinary level. For theology graduates, the College hopes to offer next year the Southampton Degree of Master of Theology.

Cranmer Hall, St John's College, Durham

St John's is a College of the University of Durham, situated close to Durham Cathedral. It is divided into two halls: Cranmer Hall, which provides training for ordained and lay ministry for both women and men; and John's Hall, where undergraduate and postgraduates study the full range of University disciplines. The halls share the College Chapel and other facilities. Evangelical in its foundation, the College also welcomes students of other traditions and has close links with Ushaw College (a Roman Catholic Seminary) and the Wesley Study Centre, many of whose students study in Cranmer Hall.

New Courses - The College has recently introduced both an Honours Degree and a certificate in Theology and Ministry which are validated by Durham University and accredited by ABM as fulfilling the Bishops' Regulations for ordination training. They have been developed ecumenically with Ushaw College and the Wesley Study Centre and provide a fully integrated course covering academic and practical theology. Included in the latter are special courses which explore Christian ministry in the urban and rural contexts, taking up the insights of *Faith in the City* and *Faith in the Countryside*.

University - Those with appropriate qualifications can include study for the BA with Honours in Theology taught in the University of Durham Department of Theology, and graduates in theology can study for the College's own Diploma in Ministerial Studies, and in certain cases a research degree in the Department of Theology.

Context - Durham offers a unique context for training, combining the resources of an academic setting with the rich variety of practical experience found in the North East of England. A well-established Urban Studies Unit in Gateshead gives focus to these opportunities.

Single and married students are given equal space to grow in their preparation for ministry; family participation is warmly welcomed in worship, courses and meals, and an active spouses' network facilitates involvement. A tutorial system ensures the personal profiling of each student's course, including their spiritual, academic and practical ministerial formation. The College seeks to work with, and enhance, students' previous experience, and to facilitate an understanding of both the content of the Gospel and the context of mission in contemporary society.

Lincoln Theological College

At Lincoln we aim to equip people for ministry in the Church. Students comprise men and women from a wide range of backgrounds and ages. Our main task is to help lay foundations for ministry upon which people can build throughout their working lives.

We draw on a wide variety of resources, including the backgrounds and experiences of students; the experience of living, working and praying together for two or three years; and our own context, in the centre of an industrial city, serving a prosperous, agricultural area and also within easy reach of the East Midlands, Humberside and South Yorkshire.

We have had women students since 1970 and Methodist students since 1985. Usually just over half of our students are married. There are numerous opportunities for spouses and families to be involved in the life of the College, if they wish. Our staff include lay people as well as Anglican clergy and a Methodist minister.

The College whilst standing in the broadly catholic tradition in the Church of England, includes people from a wide variety of traditions. The daily offices and the eucharist provide the framework for our life. People are encouraged, with the assistance of a personal tutor, to develop their own patterns of prayer and worship within this context.

Three programmes of study are available: the three-year Bachelor of Theology Honours degree in conjunction with Nottingham University is specially designed as a preparation for ministry; a two-year Certificate in Ministerial Studies for people over 30, which integrates theological study and pastoral experience in preparation for ministry; and a two-year Master of Divinity, in conjunction with Nottingham University, or Certificate in Ministry and Mission, for theology graduates, designed to build on and develop previous theological study, in preparation for ministry. Learning takes place through seminars, lectures, tutorials, group project work, a wide range of supervised placements, and reflection on the experience of learning, living and praying together.

Accommodation for single people is in bed-sitters either in the College or in nearby College houses. We have a large number of houses and flats within easy walking distance of the College, to let to married students.

College of the Resurrection, Mirfield

The College was founded by the Community of the Resurrection and a distinctive feature of the College is its association with the life of the Community in whose grounds it is situated.

The common life of the College is distinct from that of the Community but there are many contacts between the two. Members of the Community as well as the priests on the College staff, some of whom are not members of the Community, are available to give spiritual guidance to students. The day begins with matins and the Eucharist in the College chapel, and the College joins the Community in the Community Church for Evensong.

The College provides courses for graduates and non-graduates. Eight places (out of a total of 36) are reserved for married students and accommodation for them is provided within easy walking distance from the College.

Theological study is carried out within a framework provided by the common life, prayer and worship, and initiation into pastoral work. Students are encouraged to think theologically and to articulate their own understanding of the Gospel. Emphasis is placed on seminars and tuition in small groups.

All students follow courses leading to the award of the Mirfield Certificate in Pastoral Theology. Graduates in Theology and candidates over 30 complete the appropriate courses in 2 years. Candidates under 30 who have not previously graduated in Theology complete the appropriate courses in 3 years.

Graduates in subjects other than Theology whose previous degree qualifies them to read for a degree in Theology with support from central Church funds may take the Leeds BA in Theology and Religious Studies in 2 years; during these years they travel to Leeds for tuition. In their third year the remaining requirements of the Mirfield Certificate in Pastoral Theology are completed.

A member of staff with recent parish experience acts as Director of Pastoral Studies. Courses in Sociology and Psychology are given in conjunction with Pastoral Studies Units on Industrial Life and Society, Community Relations and 'Samaritans'. All students also attend a Hospital Course on 'Introduction to Health Care'.

The College is set in industrial West Yorkshire, which provides ample opportunity for practical experience as well as sufficient parishes for parochial training, mainly of a 'Urban Priority Area' nature. Considerable emphasis is placed on the importance of preaching and the communication of Christian teaching to children and adults. For the whole of the final year each student is attached to a local parish.

Oak Hill Theological College, London

Oak Hill stands in 60 acres of its own grounds, is within easy reach of Central London and 4 miles from the M25.

The evangelical ethos of Oak Hill means that the bible is at the heart of College life. We have over 100 full-time students with an academic staff of 11, who also teach on the part-time Ministerial Training Course. There is also an Extension Course.

Our academic programme is an integrated one, but within it there are many options open to meet individual needs. There is a two-year full-time course for a Dip.HE in Theological and Pastoral Studies. Many then go on to do either a BA or BA Honours Degree in the third year.

The College aims to equip students with knowledge and skills for Christian ministry, including training in preaching, teaching, pastoral counselling, evangelism and Christian leadership. Theological reflection takes place and skills are learned in supervised pastoral placements. Development of a deepening spirituality is encouraged through personal and corporate worship, and in interaction within fellowship groups and in the community as a whole.

Oak Hill attracts students from a wide range of ages and backgrounds, including students from Africa, America and Europe.

Single students have well appointed rooms, and all year occupancy is possible. College accommodation ranges from bedsits to four bedroom houses, with access for the disabled. Good facilities for children, including a creche, make it possible for wives to enter into College life.

Sports and other recreational facilities are provided.

The Queen's College, Birmingham

The College, situated on a five-acre site within a quarter of a mile of Birmingham University, is the first fully ecumenical College in Britain. The main participants are Anglicans, Methodists and the URC, but other denominations are represented. The College caters for men and women and welcomes all Church traditions. Rooms exist for 75 students and 22 flats for married students are on the campus. Spouses' and family participation in College activities and meals is encouraged.

College life has its focus in the Chapel, and the development of personal and corporate discipleship is a major priority. Living, worshipping and exploring mission in a varied community adds its own positive dimension, enabling exploration of the riches and contributions of different traditions. Daily worship (including the eucharist), reflects the traditions represented in the College as well as the special challenge of its ecumenical character.

Many ordinands include a Birmingham University course in their training, a BA Honours in Theology, a two-year BD (for graduates in non-theological subjects), a Diploma in Pastoral Studies, MA, M.Phil, Ph.D (for Theology graduates). Queen's itself offers a two-year Diploma and a University validated B.Th degree, access to which can be gained by a sufficient standard in the first year foundation course.

Birmingham is an ideal city to discover and face numerous pertinent questions and provides varied opportunities for practical experience. Considerable use is made of local resources, enabling contextual learning. Various courses have particular relevance and immediacy in a multi-cultural setting.

A month's course on the eucharist is done jointly with a Roman Catholic College and there is a Black Christian Studies Course. Participation is possible, too, in some Selly Oak courses. A few students spend a year in Handsworth (5 miles from College) integrating theology and involvement in both local church and secular life. Links outside include Colleges in Germany, India and South Africa.

Cohesion in community is assisted by teams of staff and students, by reflection groups and individual tutorials. Living together and facing many issues in free enquiry and creative tension develop a deeper awareness of what it means to be the body of Christ.

Ridley Hall - Cambridge Federation

Ridley Hall trains up to 60 men and women for ordained ministry in the Church of England. It is part of the Cambridge Federation of Theological Colleges.

Ridley Hall was opened in 1881 and was named after the Reformation leader Bishop Nicholas Ridley. It bears witness to a tradition which is evangelical, comprehensive, scholarly and practical.

Ridley is **evangelical** in the College's commitment to the central Gospel reality of God's redemption in Jesus Christ, the Church's task of mission and evangelism, and the authority of the Bible. It fosters a thoroughly biblical faith which engages honestly with critical issues.

Ridley is **comprehensive** in its insistence that the rich diversity of the Anglican communion and the worldwide Church should be valued, explored and understood. Students from other traditions are very welcome and make a full contribution. Involvement in the teaching, worshipping and social life of the Federation enables students to train in an ecumenical context, while remaining rooted in the ethos of their own particular college.

Ridley is **scholarly** in its commitment to seeking after truth. It provides an intellectually stretching environment in which to study theology. Graduates with a good first degree may read for Part II of the University Theological and Religious Studies Tripos. Others take the Certificate in Theology for Ministry, a Federation-taught course which is validated by the University Divinity Faculty. A wide range of courses is on offer and every effort is made to tailor a programme to individuals' particular needs and interests.

Ridley is **practical** in its concern to equip students to engage creatively with a world which is torn, needy and very much the object of God's love. It links the study of theology closely to the practice of ministry. The Mission and Pastoral Studies programme consists of a great variety of courses and practical experience, including involvement for all students in one two-week parish mission.

A feature of theological College life unique to Ridley is the 'God on Monday' Project. This consists of a programme of residential seminar and personal study weeks for leaders in business, commerce and industry. Engagement with this helps ordinands to become better equipped for ministry to and with people in business, and with lay Christians generally.

Ripon College, Cuddesdon

The College is the result of a merger in 1975 between two Colleges: Cuddesdon - a College in the catholic tradition - and Ripon Hall - in the modernist and liberal tradition. Students today, however, are drawn from across the theological spectrum. It is in no sense a party College and most students are anxious to explore a range of spiritualities and theologies.

The College is situated in a village seven miles from Oxford but has houses in Oxford and Sheffield. There are about seventy students and seven staff resident at any one time. Single students live in the College and married students and their families in bungalows and flats on the campus or in the village.

The work of the College falls into four principal areas, reflecting the need for spiritual formation, theological education, pastoral practice and ministerial skills:

1. Worship is at the heart of each day. The daily offices are said and there is a (voluntary) daily eucharist. In addition, students are encouraged to put together and lead their own acts of special worship. Students also have attachments at local churches where they lead worship and preach.

2. Rigorous theological learning is encouraged and the College has good links with the University from which many students will obtain a qualification - degree, certificate or diploma. There are good and growing links with two other Anglican Colleges and with the United Reformed Church ordinands at Mansfield College. The College shares a Lutheran lecturer with Mansfield.

3. In recent years there has been an increasing emphasis on applied theology. As well as formal teaching in pastoral psychology and theology, students have attachments with secular agencies - hospital, school, hospice, prison, and so on. In addition, all students spend four weeks of one long vacation on placement in an English parish. In recent years there has been a particular emphasis on learning how to reflect theologically in these various situations.

4. Many single students will also spend several months training in an urban priority area parish in Sheffield, learning how to use the theology they are acquiring in an area deeply alienated from traditional Christianity. Here, the missionary and evangelistic challenge facing the contemporary church is most clearly to be seen.

The College has three terms of ten weeks and prospective candidates are encouraged to visit and stay - normally from tea-time on Thursday (4 pm) to Saturday morning.

St John's College, Nottingham

St John's has over 90 Church of England ordinands and up to 30 people who come from other denominations or other countries or who are preparing for lay ministry. It is committed to the development of women's ministry in the Church and currently 24 of its 120 students and four of its thirteen full-time teaching staff are women.

The College occupies its own campus near Nottingham University. Many students undertake the Honours B.Th degree (three years for non-graduates, two years for gradates) which is partly taught in the University. The University also validates the College's MA in the Theology of Mission and Ministry which is open to theology graduates, and to other graduates as the final year of their time at College. The College offers Diploma courses for two-year candidates; a range of other opportunities for postgraduate study is also available. Most students have opportunity to take part in an urban training project in Urban Priority Areas in Nottingham.

The College has accommodation for single and married students, available for the whole year, but housing is cheap in the area and many married people buy their own houses. Spouses and families are welcome to play as full a part in College life as they wish. There is a lively and caring (but self-critical) sense of community at the College, an important focus of which is daily worship in chapel and twice-weekly fellowship groups.

St John's belongs to the evangelical tradition of the Church of England and has been influenced by the charismatic movement; it also seeks to be open to learning from different sources and has members of other traditions and other denominations among teaching staff and students. The College's aim is to enable students from all backgrounds to fulfil its motto - St Paul's words: 'Woe to me if I do not preach the Gospel' - by encouraging them to learn about the bible, to face hard questions about the faith, to deepen their understanding of the world in which they live and the people to whom they preach, to reflect on their own experience in the light of the bible and theology, and to grow in their relationship to God.

St Stephen's House, Oxford

St Stephen's House stands firmly within the catholic tradition of the Church of England. It prepares candidates for ministry from other parts of the Anglican Communion (especially, at present, the USA and the Church in Wales) but the great majority of our candidates are preparing to be priests and deacons in England.

Our buildings are often called Oxford's best-kept secret. Until 1980 they were the monastery of the Society of St John the Evangelist. Tucked behind the multi-cultural shops and terraced houses of East Oxford, St Stephen's House incorporates a set of very beautiful monastic buildings, a fine Victorian church, and modern student and staff housing, all set in attractive gardens. Families of married students (about ⅓ of the College are married) are encouraged to worship with the College and neighbouring parishioners on Sundays in St John's church, and to take a lively part in College life.

St Stephen's House caters for the whole range of students, non-graduates and graduates, some with years of work experience, some straight from higher education, yet others from the Aston Training Scheme. Many undertake courses run by Oxford University while they are here, the degree course in Theology for those academically qualified already, or either the two or three-year Oxford Certificate in theology. But all, whether or not on a university course, have access to Oxford's libraries, and may attend lectures in the University.

Those without an academic background will undertake a Theological College Certificate course. Because we are a relatively small College (no more than sixty students) we are able to tailor courses to candidates' particular abilities and previous experience. Whatever route a person follows, we are keen to stress the centrality of pastoral experience. Our situation in East Oxford gives us access to a very wide range of parish and other placements, from airport and prison chaplaincies to work with the single homeless or mentally handicapped.

The life of prayer is central to all that we do, and so we value our close link with the contemplative community of Anglican nuns at Fairacres.

Salisbury and Wells Theological College

The College community is remarkably diverse. It includes men and women, single and married (many with young families), who are drawn from all types of social and academic backgrounds. Together, they represent the widest possible variety of traditions in the Church. There are Evangelicals, Anglo-Catholics, liberals and conservatives. There are students with O levels and CSEs, and others with Ph.Ds. There are army officers and ambulance drivers, stockbrokers and journalists, those who were brought up in Urban Priority Areas, some in their early twenties, and a few in their mid-fifties.

Students over thirty follow a two-year course leading to a Diploma in Christian Ministry, while those under thirty study for a Bachelor of Theology Degree, or a Certificate in Theology. All the courses receive University validation, but they are far more than explorations of academic theology. Everything in the courses is geared towards preparing people for ordained ministry, and each of them gives ample opportunity to learn through experience. All the courses include a six week placement with a secular agency in an urban or rural setting. Theology graduates have a number of options open to them. Some will find the Diploma the most appropriate course, while others will require specially designed courses.

The management structure of the College, and our expectations of one another, reflect the fact that everyone has already had significant experience. All decisions are taken in working groups of students and staff. There is no imposition of rules and regulations. Students are asked to work out their own rule of life and to discuss it with the other members of their College group, in order to learn how to create appropriate disciplines for which they are properly accountable.

This model of preparation for ministry is inspired by an understanding of the minister as a servant of the people of God, not as a man or woman in charge; and by a vision of a God whose sense of adventure and humility are both disconcerting and exhilarating.

Trinity College, Bristol

Trinity College, founded in October 1971, takes forward the task of theological education first begun in Bristol in the 1920s. Its campus is pleasantly situated in an eight-acre park on the edge of the Bristol Downs, about two miles from the city centre. In the last few years there have been extensive new additions to the College plant, providing a superb facility both for residential and part-time courses for ministerial training.

Trinity is evangelical by tradition and co-educational by foundation. It aims to create an environment in which men and women preparing for Christian service and ordained ministry are given help and encouragement to think biblically and at the same time face the full force of the contemporary situation in current objections to the Christian faith. All students are encouraged to view spiritual and personal development as an integral part of their time at College. A significant number of students come from the overseas Church, thus giving Trinity a strongly inter-denominational and international flavour.

Trinity's courses include: the Diploma of Higher Education in Religious Studies, BA and BA(Hons) Degrees in Theological Studies - two and three-year courses validated by the Council for National Academic Awards (CNAA) and recognised by ABM as meeting the requirements for training men and women for ministry. There are a number of one-year courses on offer. Students may also pursue studies towards Bristol University MA, M.Litt and Ph.D degrees and higher degrees awarded by CNAA, or one of the two MAs taught jointly with the Cheltenham and Gloucester College of Higher Education. The College has an Urban Studies Centre based in the West Midlands where some students can work in placements for part of their course.

Trinity attempts to place a special emphasis on community life, including the integration of single and married students with families into the life of the College. Wives are encouraged to take part in College courses and training. The emphasis on pastoral care within the community and spiritual growth within the individual is focused on the centrally important group life of the whole College.

Westcott House - Cambridge Federation

Since its foundation in 1881, Westcott House, situated in the centre of Cambridge, has been closely associated with the University. Since 1972 it has been part of a Federation, the other three members of which are Ridley Hall (Anglican), Wesley House (Methodist) and Westminster College (URC). The Federation involves a long-term and developing commitment one to another, and also the possibility of new ecumenical commitments, involving other parts of the Christian Church. Through it, students have constant opportunities to learn of the faith of others, as well as to deepen themselves in the tradition of their own House. Westcott House itself stands for an inclusive catholicism, and welcomes into its membership students from all shades of opinion within Anglicanism. Each College in the Federation is responsible for the selection and pastoral care of its own students, but most of the teaching is shared between the Colleges, and there is a weekly Eucharist presided over in turn by each of the four Colleges, at which the Federation worships together.

Membership of the House is open to women as well as men, and since 1982 there have been two women amongst the staff of six. The House is committed to the use of inclusive language in its worship, as far as this is possible. Twice daily worship centred round the offices is at the centre of the College's life. Spouses of married members are welcome to play as full a part in the life and worship of the community as they wish.

All ordinands at Westcott work for the Certificate in Theology for Ministry, issued by the Faculty of Theology. As part of their training, graduates with a '2:1' or first class degree may read for Part II of the University's Theology Tripos. Theology graduates may be eligible to read for the University's Diploma, or M.Phil. All members have access to the University Library, the Graduate Centre and other University facilities, and may attend University lectures for a small fee.

Westcott House rents a house in Ancoats, Manchester, where small groups of students (also from the Federation) spend up to three months working at their theology in the context of practical involvement in the urban world.

There are three terms a year of ten weeks each. Parish placements etc. take place in the vacation. Single students normally live in Westcott itself, and there is provision for those who have no other home to stay in the House during the vacation. There are also nine flats for married students on the site.

Wycliffe Hall, Oxford

Wycliffe Hall belongs to the Evangelical tradition in the Church of England. It therefore aims to teach an essentially biblical approach to theology and ministry, with the gospel of redemption at the heart of its theology and the evangelistic and missionary task of the Church as the focus of its training.

The Hall welcomes men and women of various outlooks, however, and encourages an honest search for truth in the context of good scholarship and living faith.

Situated within ten minutes walk of the centre of the city and of the University area, the Hall offers ready access to University lectures, libraries, etc. Students also enjoy the rich cultural, social and religious life of Oxford. We enjoy close relations with the other theological Colleges in Oxford, particularly St Stephen's House and Ripon College, Cuddesdon, with whom we arrange joint teaching and worship on a regular basis.

The student body is usually between 80 and 90. About 80% are Church of England ordinands, but an international and ecumenical flavour is ensured by the presence of students from other countries, some already ordained, and a number engaged in theological research. Married students live in houses and flats owned by the Hall, unless they prefer to provide their own accommodation. Students' wives and husbands are welcome at all Hall activities, including meals; children are welcome to lunch. There is a programme specifically for wives, and an evening class programme which many spouses find helpful.

There are three main courses available (with further options for those who already have a degree in theology). The Oxford University Certificate in Theology can be taken in either three or two years, and includes all requirements for ordination. Wycliffe Hall's own Diploma covers similar ground, but is assessed by essays and other project work not by examination. Graduates with a high class in a previous degree may take the Oxford University BA in Theology in two years, followed by a year of Certificate papers to complete ordination requirements.

The Theological Institute of the Scottish Episcopal Church, Coates Hall

There are two major factors which distinguish Coates Hall from other Colleges and which interest English candidates: the position of the **Anglican Church in Scotland** (of which the Institute is the main training institution) and the College's links with the University of Edinburgh.

The Scottish Episcopal Church, unlike the Church of England, is neither the established church, nor the church of the majority. In this it resembles most provinces of the Anglican Church. The Institute has close links with local parishes, and plays a significant role within the province: ordinands here stand to learn something of the nature of Anglicanism not easily gained in England.

The Institute also works closely with the **Divinity Faculty of Edinburgh University (New College)**. This faculty, which is one of the largest in Britain, has an international reputation and attracts staff and students from across the world. Although a training institution for the (Presbyterian) Church of Scotland, staff come from a number of traditions (including Roman Catholic and Anglican) and the presence of our students is greatly valued. Suitably qualified candidates may take courses leading to the BD and M.Th (details on request).

The University courses include pastoral work, but Coates Hall provides additional pastoral training to meet the needs of the Anglican ministry, especially through work with local parishes. The Episcopal Church is fully committed to a developing programme of urban mission, and Edinburgh offers a very fruitful opportunity to share in that and learn from it.

There is a strong liturgical life within Coates Hall, but because it belongs to the whole Scottish province, it is not a party college. There is a regular pattern of daily prayer and an annual retreat. Within this framework, each is encouraged to discover his or her own pattern of spirituality.

Coates Hall is in the centre of Edinburgh. It is a small College, but enlarged by the participation of families. Single students live in College, and there are flats available for those who are married.

St Michael and All Angels' Theological College, Llandaff, Cardiff, Wales

Courses: The College makes full use of the facilities provided by the Collegiate Faculty of Theology of the University of Wales College of Cardiff and of the pastoral opportunities offered by local parishes, hospitals, Urban Priority Areas and secular agencies. The main course for those under 30 is the University of Wales Bachelor of Theology while those over 30 read for the College's Diploma in Ministerial Studies. Graduates in Theology read the Diploma in Pastoral Studies and there are also Masters degrees in Theology available. There are no extra charges involved for pursuing any of these University courses.

Objectives of Training: The College believes that these are implicit in the Bishop's Declaration to the candidates in the Ordinal of the Alternative

Services Book 1980 (pages 344 and 356). The rationale of the College Syllabus with its aims and objectives is based upon three fundamental growth points in holiness, discernment and responsibility. This demonstrates the College's commitment to the training of ordained ministers to serve the Church into the next millennium, leading and serving the People of God in their mission to the world. The central focus of corporate worship, the challenge of community life, the rigour of academic study informed by its emphasis on pastoral care and involvement in the contemporary Church and society through parish links and placements all aim at producing men and women of God, holy, discerning and responsible in their ministry to and with the People of God.

Practicalities: The College has room for 40 Ordinands, both men and women. There are also 6 flats in the College and there are houses available for families within easy walking distance of the College. There are five members of staff and the College has a strong connection with the South Wales Baptist College, whose staff also contribute to much of the teaching at the University. The College sings Evensong at the Cathedral each Wednesday evening. Cardiff itself is one of the finest cities in Britain, has a huge University complex of 9,000 students of which Theology and Religious Studies make up 200. There are many excellent local schools. The city has a great range of cultural and sporting activities. Cardiff is one hour and fifty minutes by train from London.

PART-TIME COURSES

Canterbury School of Ministry

Canterbury School of Ministry developed out of work originally undertaken at St Augustine's College, Canterbury. Candidates are prepared for stipendiary, non-stipendiary or lay ministry by means of a three-year part-time course in Pastoral and Theological Studies. Emphasis is laid upon the integration of theological study with the secular experience of the students, and personal tuition with this in view is given to each student.

Each year's corporate programme comprises 32 weekly seminars, seven weekend conferences, one study day, a weekend retreat and a nine-day Summer School. Husbands and wives, and families are invited to attend the Summer School and also regular social and educational events. The meetings take place in Canterbury, tutorial supervision is available through the dioceses of Canterbury and Rochester.

Though funded and supported by the diocese of Canterbury, the governing body is ecumenical in membership, and also includes representatives of the University of Kent at Canterbury and Christ Church College of Higher Education. The Course is open to applicants who are seeking ordination in any denomination, and to lay people who are looking for an intensive course in Pastoral Theology and preparation for ministry.

Carlisle Diocesan Training Institute

The Carlisle Diocesan Training Institute (CDTI) began its life in October, 1978, as a pilot scheme to train ordinands from the Diocese of Carlisle. This diocese covers the vast 2,500 square miles of Cumbria which has an often scattered population of just under half a million people. Both geography and demography contributed to the felt need for a local non-residential course of training.

Since then candidates from adjoining areas of the neighbouring dioceses of Blackburn and Bradford have looked to CDTI for training, as have a local candidates from the Methodist and United Reformed Churches. So too have lay men and women. And in 1990 Readers in training in the Carlisle Diocese also joined the Course. Ordination candidates train for both stipendiary and non-stipendiary ministry.

Training takes place over three years, each of which is divided into three terms. It combines local group tutorials, residential weekends at Rydal Hall near Ambleside and an annual summer school at Durham, Edinburgh or York with parish and specialist placements to form a coherent pattern of training. The tutorials are held fortnightly at venues and times to suit each group. Tutors are local. Consultants and lecturers are drawn at present from the Universities of Durham, Edinburgh, Lancaster, Manchester and Newcastle.

The Institute logo, designed by staff and students, so arranges and superimposes the CDTI initials as to portray a divided world held together by the cross. The Latin phrase, *Securus Te Projice*, quoting St Augustine, invites those who enter to come in with full abandon to experience the joy and freedom of living and learning as Christians together.

East Anglian Ministerial Training Course

The East Anglian Ministerial Training Course (EAMTC) is a part-time Course preparing men and women over 30 years of age for stipendiary and non-stipendiary ministry. It serves the dioceses of Ely, Norwich, St Edmundsbury and Ipswich, Chelmsford and neighbouring dioceses as the need arises. It offers a three-year course of 'ministerial formation', enabling the student to acquire theological knowledge and pastoral skills and to continue his or her personal development. Students are normally expected to complete the full three years.

Theological study takes place on two fronts: 1. By weekly tutorials under the supervision of a local tutor, using study-unit material of a kind similar to that used by the Open University. 2. At 7 residential weekends and an 8-day Summer School in each year and where, besides further work in biblical studies and doctrine, training is given in prayer and spirituality, sermon preparation and pastoral skills. Academic assessment is by essays. The student's personal development as an ordinand is also monitored and assessed.

Students come from varied backgrounds and bring a diversity of experience to the Course. EAMTC tries to help students to reflect theologically upon their experience and to test their theological ideas in the light of it.

Social events involving wives and husbands of those in training are held regularly.

East Midlands Ministry Training Course

The East Midlands Ministry Training Course (EMMTC) offers a three-year part-time course for both lay and ordained ministry. It serves the dioceses of Derby, Leicester, Lincoln and Southwell.

It currently trains candidates for stipendiary and non-stipendiary ministry as priests, deacons and accredited lay ministers. In addition, a number of lay people use the course to equip themselves for lay ministry. Students represent a wide spectrum of tradition, having great diversity in educational background, and hold different visions of their future ministry. Although predominantly Anglican, the Course is open to students from any Christian denomination, and currently includes ordinands from the Methodist and United Reformed Churches as well as lay people from Roman Catholic,

Baptist and Society of Friends. This diversity is also reflected on the panel of part-time tutors.

The Course is based in the Adult Education Department of Nottingham University. It is thus in a favourable position to draw upon the skills and insights which help mature adults to become learners. Teaching staff are drawn from the University Departments of Theology and Education, and from a variety of institutions in the East Midlands. Particular attention is paid to the involvement of students' families who are invited to join in residential Summer Schools and certain other occasions.

The Course, which leads to a Diploma in Theological and Pastoral Studies, of the University of Nottingham, has no formal examinations; a student's progress is monitored by continuous assessment.

Gloucester School for Ministry

Founded in 1964, the Gloucester School for Ministry is a part-time Course for ordinands from the Dioceses of Gloucester and Hereford, together with a small number from neighbouring dioceses. It also accepts students from the United Reformed Church and the Methodist Church. Students attend on two evenings each week at either Gloucester or Ludlow during the three eight-week terms. There are also two residential weekends each term, and a ten-day Summer School in August.

The Course has recently been radically revised to ensure a close relationship between academic and practical work. Student-led seminars form an important part of the Course, and follow a thematic approach to draw together various strands of learning and experience. Students take part in a social placement and a parish placement.

Emphasis is placed on the importance of the group as a training for collaborative ministry.

It is planned to open a third teaching centre in Bristol in 1992.

North East Ordination Course

Founded in 1976, the North East Ordination Course (NEOC) serves the Anglican dioceses of Newcastle, Durham, York and Ripon, the Northern province of the United Reformed Church and the Methodist Church.

NEOC trains men and women who are sponsored or recommended for ordained or accredited ministry, stipendiary and non-stipendiary. There are no formal academic requirements, and members come from a diversity of traditions and educational backgrounds.

For most candidates the Course lasts three years and consists of three parallel elements:

1. Residential periods (an eight-day Summer School and six weekends in each year) in which members share the experience of living, praying and studying together, and work in groups to relate to each other the various elements of their training.

2. Practical projects, usually one based on members' existing experience of work and daily life, and another attached to a parish or specialised chaplaincy providing experience in a less familiar context.

3. Weekly tutorials and private study, through which knowledge and understanding are gained of the basic disciplines of theology.

Candidates are assessed by a variety of methods including self-assessment, reports, projects with pastoral application, as well as more formal essays and biblical exegeses.

Each member has a Chaplain with whom he or she can discuss in confidence general matters about the Course, and personal and ministerial development. Chaplaincy is also intended to help members to examine the impact of their training on relationships at home, at work and in their own churches; they are encouraged to form Chaplaincy Groups, which include representatives of all these areas of their lives.

Northern Ordination Course

Established in 1970 by the dioceses of Chester, Blackburn, Liverpool and Manchester, the Northern Ordination Course (NOC) is now also sponsored by the dioceses of York, Bradford, Ripon, Sheffield and Wakefield. It trains men and women for ordained and lay ministries in the Church of England as well as in the Methodist and United Reformed Churches, both stipendiary and non-stipendiary. The Course may also admit private students.

The Course is based on nine residential week-end conferences and an 8-day Summer School held in each of three years in Manchester. In addition each student attends a weekly evening meeting at the nearest centre, Liverpool, Manchester or Leeds. In addition about 10 hours of private study per week is required.

Assessment of progress is through continuous appraisal of academic, pastoral and personal development, and also through external assessment of extended essays and projects. The Course seeks to relate theological understanding closely to the practicalities of ministry as well as to the realities of secular life.

Most of the students are aged between 30 and 45 although there is no upper age limit. The Course tries to use experience of life as a basis for theological reflection.

The ecumenical nature of the Course itself and its association with the Northern Federation for Ministerial Training makes it a good forum for exploring the nature of Christian ministry across the denominations.

There are three full-time members of staff and four part-time.

Oak Hill Ministerial Training Course

The Oak Hill Ministerial Training Course (MTC) is a three-year part-time Course. It is based at Oak Hill College, which can be reached from the London Underground network (Southgate station) or the M25 (three miles from junction 24).

Students attend on twenty-eight Tuesday evenings, eight residential weekends and a one-week residential summer school in each academic year.

A typical Tuesday evening's programme begins with worship and a meal, and includes two hour-long learning sessions separated by a break for coffee. Residential weekends (which run from Friday evening until Sunday lunchtime) aim to take a selected subject from the evening class curriculum to a greater depth. Two of these occasions are open to married students' partners.

The full-time Oak Hill staff provide most of the tuition, but visiting lecturers are regularly invited to contribute their specialist knowledge and experience.

Practical training is monitored by a large number of Pastoral Supervisors, most of whom are vicars and ministers of local churches. Students are required to complete the two placements (one in a church and the other in a secular setting) during their time on the Course.

Each MTC student has a study-bedroom in the College, for his or her exclusive use on Tuesday evenings and during residential weekends.

MTC members have full borrowing rights from the Oak Hill library. There is also an MTC Resource Room with its own book collection, sets of lecture tapes and refreshment facilities.

Oxford Ministry Course

The Oxford Ministry Course offers a comprehensive theological education and training to prepare candidates for a ministry through the Church to the world.

The Course meets in year groups for three nine-week terms each year. Lectures are on an evening weekday basis; there are two residential weekends each term and a ten-day period of residence in the summer.

Lecturers are drawm from the three Oxford theological Colleges, the diocesan staff and the Course staff.

At present there is a fairly even balance between women and men students and from next year the Course will be ecumenical with the inclusion of students from the United Reformed Church.

Many candidates take the Certificate in Biblical and Theological Studies offered by the Department for Continuing Education of the University of Oxford, while some do special courses.

All take part in the worship of the course, group work, pastoral placements, seminars and workshops, as well as attendance at lectures.

We are conscious of the need for sensitivity towards the families of those in training and the importance of strong links between the Course and the parish to which ordinands belong.

St Albans Diocese Ministerial Training Scheme

The St Albans Diocese Ministerial Training Scheme provides a three-year part-time course which trains men and women for a variety of different ministries, lay and ordained. Many candidates continue their exploration of vocation while they are studying on the Course.

The Course provides opportunities to develop appropriate personal qualities, understanding and skills for ministry today. The programme links study of experience in today's world with exploration of the Bible and Christian tradition. The experiential learning component of the Course is set alongside more traditional teaching methods. Students use their own experience before the Course as an important resource, to be drawn on as they learn from tutors and from each other.

Students are required to attend two evenings a week during term-time, and each evening includes a meal and worship, as well as teaching. There are five residential weekends each year and an eight-day summer school in August, and students are expected to spend some time each week on reading and assignments.

There are two full-time and three half-time staff, and the Course is able to make use of local tutors to help with teaching and the supervision of placements. A local panel and personal tutor assist each student's own development and ensure that training relates to their home situations.

Southern Dioceses Ministerial Training Scheme

The Southern Dioceses Ministerial Training Scheme (SDMTS) provides a part-time course based in Salisbury. Training is offered for stipendiary and non-stipendiary ministry to women and men sponsored for ordination by their dioceses. We also train those preparing for ordained ministry in the Methodist and United Reformed Churches.

We cater for candidates from our sponsoring dioceses: Bath and Wells, Bristol, Chichester, Portsmouth, Salisbury and Winchester, and receive candidates from other neighbouring diocese where appropriate. Training lasts for three years.

Students spend up to fifteen hours a week in study under the guidance of a local tutor using material prepared by the Course staff. Students are normally attached to a small tutorial group for the duration of their training. In addition there are up to six residential weekends and one eight-day summer school in each year of training. The residential periods supplement the academic work of the tutorials with a great emphasis on pastoral theology, spirituality and personal growth.

As well as covering the usual academic theology components, the Course places a high value on relating theological study to the students own situation in the local community, the Church and, where appropriate, in secular employment.

Members of SDMTS are also full members of Salisbury and Wells Theological College and are able to take advantage of the facilities of the College as well as the opportunity to spend additional periods in the College where appropriate.

Southwark Ordination Course

The Southwark Ordination Course trains men and women recommended for ordained ministry, stipendiary and non-stipendiary and candidates sponsored by the Methodist Church and the United Reformed Church. Members who come from London and the surrounding counties represent a wide spectrum of traditions and hold different visions of their future ministry. As most are in secular employment during training, they will constantly be provoked into relating their theological insights to the contexts of everyday work and life.

The purpose of the Course is to help prepare men and women together for ministry in church and society enabling them in their various contexts to grow in their knowledge and love of God through Jesus Christ, to identify and respond to manifestations of God's rule of love and justice, and so to play their part as ordained persons in the mission of God.

Each year contains seven residential weekends; one or more study days; a nine-day residential summer school; one evening class each week for three ten-week terms; an annual 'running' project; the personal prayer and private study that members are expected to do on their own; tutorial consultations. Together they address different contexts - home, classroom, short and longer periods of residence away from home, studying alone and working with others. This pattern recognises that members' future ministries will be exercised in different settings and seeks to prepare them for such diverse challenges.

There is an annual weekend and other meetings for members' partners.

South-West Ministerial Training Course

The South-West Ministerial Training Course (SWMTC) serves the Dioceses of Exeter and Truro which are virtually coterminous with the counties of Devon and Cornwall.

The training is part-time and extends over three years. The programme comprises lecture/seminar courses, private tutorials, pastoral placements, residential weekends and Summer Schools. The seven residential weekends per year are based in Exeter whilst the Summer Schools are located at a range of venues outside the region.

Assessment is by a variety of assignments including essays, seminar presentations and project work. The Exeter University Certificate in Theology is an integral part of our syllabus and assessment programme.

The Course trains men and women for stipendiary and non-stipendiary ministries on behalf of the Anglican, Methodist and United Reformed Churches. The syllabus is structured around three key words: Being, Knowing and Doing. Candidates are helped to deepen their knowledge of the biblical/theological foundations of their faith, and to acquire appropriate ministerial skills. But above all, they will be encouraged to develop greater self-awareness and spiritual depth so that knowledge and ability are allied to appropriate attitudes and personal integrity.

The educational style is as appropriate to the development of adults with a premium placed on individual responsibility and self-assessment. We also seek to honour the individuality of candidates with respect to background, context and future ministerial expectations.

West Midlands Ministerial Training Course

The West Midlands Ministerial Training Course (WMMTC) is ecumenical and is based at Queen's College, Birmingham. It lasts three years, and is intended primarily to serve part-time students in the West Midlands who have been recommended for training by a recognised Church body. Private students are also admitted with local recommendations. Students wishing to attend for particular parts of the Course can be considered for membership, eg. just Tuesday evenings. The Course aims to affirm the students' recent and present experience; exemptions from parts of the Course are considered where appropriate. Both men and women train on the Course.

Training together is crucial to the Course, and the fellowship, mutual support and learning from one another, and worshipping together, are significant aspects. The training aims to give a balance between the essential understanding of the tradition which a student inherits, and the integrating of this into the needs of ministry in his or her particular context. Therefore, much attention is given to taking seriously the context of the West Midlands with its great variety of possibilities. In each year students and staff meet together for 32 Tuesday evenings, 7 weekends and some Sundays. Some weekends are held in other parts of the West Midlands to emphasis this regional base. The major residential session is placed before or after Easter. Students' wives or husbands and children are invited to share in the training as they wish and whenever it is convenient. The Course seeks to balance personal experience, current context, the Christian tradition, skills for ministry, and openness to self, others, and God.

Each student has a local tutor, and a tutor from the College staff who oversees their whole course. Also, where possible, students are encouraged to have a spiritual director or other guidance available to them in the course of training.

Assessment is by a variety of means; written, oral and in practical experience. The aim of the Course is to provide appropriate assessment for the wide variety of students on the Course, and for the needs of the Church for ministry today.

APPENDIX A

Paper prepared by the Initial Ministerial Education Committee of the Advisory Board of Ministry

EDUCATIONAL DEVELOPMENTS IN TRAINING FOR THE ORDAINED MINISTRY

INTRODUCTION

In the last five years, there have been fundamental changes in training for ordained ministry in the Church of England. These have taken place largely as a result of the implementation of ACCM Paper No.22, entitled *Education for the Church's Ministry*.

The first section of this paper provides background information on current ordinands and their formation. The second section introduces ACCM Paper No.22. The third section outlines the impact of the new procedures which have been introduced since 1986, following approval of ACCM Paper No.22. The fourth section summarises some of the significance of these changes in theological education.

I. BACKGROUND INFORMATION ON CURRENT ORDINANDS AND THEIR FORMATION

A) Institutions Formally Recognised in the Church of England for Ordination Training

The Church of England formally recognises a range of theological Colleges which offer training largely on the basis of three academic terms a year, with a period of between four and six weeks in placements during "vacations". It also recognises a national network of part-time training in theological Courses, where the training takes place largely through weekly tutorial groups, supplemented by between five and nine residential weekends each year and an annual summer school of between seven and fifteen days. In addition, ordinands training in Courses undertake reading, study and private prayer, an additional time commitment estimated at between 8 and 10 hours per week (1).

Men and women sponsored for non-stipendiary ministry normally train part-time in the theological Courses. Many of these candidates are continuing with secular work.

B) Ordinands

It is often suggested that most ordinands are aged under 30, single and entering training directly from higher education. This is no longer the case.

In 1991, 47.8% of the men recommended for training as stipendiary priests were aged 30 or over. 71.8% of women recommended for training as stipendiary deacons were aged 30 or over. Candidates for non-stipendiary ministry are normally aged 30 or over at the time of their entry to training.

On the whole, women are older than men when they attend selection conferences. A far lower proportion of women than of men in their early and mid-twenties offer for ordained ministry. There is an *increasing* trend towards older candidates amongst the women (2).

In 1991, approximately 16% of ordinands training in Colleges were women, whereas women comprised approximately 55% of ordinands training in Courses. A higher proportion of women who are candidates for stipendiary ministry aged over 30 choose to train part-time in Courses rather than full-time in Colleges, in some cases due to the fact that they are married and mobility is limited by their spouse's employment and family factors (3).

The number of ordinands training in theological Colleges declined from approximately 1,400 in the early 1960s to approximately 760 in the 1990s. However, the number of **married** ordinands has remained much the same (4). The proportion of married ordinands in full-time training at Colleges has more than doubled to about 55%.

These statistics suggest that an increasing emphasis in training has had to be on teaching, finance and accommodation for older men and women, some married and with family responsibilities and some single (5).

C) Formation: Colleges and Courses

The Bishops' Regulations for Training require that candidates *aged under 30* are normally sponsored for stipendiary ministry and normally required to train full-time in a theological College. If they are not already theological graduates, they normally undertake a three-year course of training. Of these candidates, 254 were reading for a degree in theology in 1990.

The situation is more complex for candidates *aged over 30*. Candidates aged over 30 may be sponsored either for non-stipendiary (6) or stipendiary ministry. If they are sponsored for stipendiary ministry, they may either train for two years full-time in a theological College or for three years part-time on a theological Course. Candidates aged under 50 who are sponsored for non-stipendiary ministry are normally expected to undertake three years of part-time theological training on a Course.

In the year 1991-92, the statistics for those undertaking training in Colleges and Courses for stipendiary and non-stipendiary ministry were as follows:

Candidates	Training in Colleges	Training in Courses	Total
Stipendiary women	110	49	159
Stipendiary men	639	46	685
Non-stipend. women	5	129	134
Non-stipend. men	6	139	145

In 1991-92 there were 61 ordinands undertaking pre-theological training with the Aston Training Scheme or the Simon of Cyrene Theological Institute. These candidates for stipendiary ministry will proceed into initial ministerial training once they have satisfactorily completed the pre-theological course.

There were also 7 candidates in training for nationally accredited lay ministry and four candidates training in Courses for local non-stipendiary ministry. In the Church of England there are also four formally recognised diocesan schemes for LNSM candidates. The development of LNSM is fully discussed in *Local NSM* (7).

A far higher **proportion** of the women sponsored for ministry than of the men are sponsored for non-stipendiary as distinct from stipendiary ministry. The survey reported in *Deacons Now* shows that bishops are most reluctant to sponsor for stipendiary ministry any candidate who cannot readily move to take up employment, especially married women (8).

II. ACCM PAPER NO.22: *EDUCATION FOR THE CHURCH'S MINISTRY*

Education for the Church's Ministry was a Report given approval by the House of Bishops in May, 1986. It was published in January, 1987, as ACCM Occasional Paper No.22, and implemented by ACCM in liaison with the theological Colleges and Courses.

The Report had, as a starting point, the far-reaching changes in the provision of ministerial training and education which had taken place in the previous 15 years. The central syllabus for theological training previously found in the General Ministerial Examination no longer provided a common basis of training for ordained ministry (9). There was increasing cooperation of theological Colleges and Courses with each other, with non-Anglican Colleges, and with Universities or the Council for National Academic Awards (CNAA), in setting up alternative educational programmes recognised by ACCM. Only one out of the 16 Colleges by then offered the General Ministerial Examination as its basic programme for ordination candidates aged under 30, while seven Colleges and five of the 14 part-time Courses offered equivalents instead of the General Ministerial Examination.

New equivalents were in many respects more appropriate for theological training in the changed circumstances of the 1980s.

The Working Party which produced the Report strongly recommended to the House of Bishops that these recent developments should be made the basis of a renewed coherence, sense of purpose and balance of responsibilities in ministerial training as a whole (10). The Report sought to find ways in which to re-establish a common basis for theological training, through assisting Colleges and Courses to arrive at common aims and to participate in a common form of monitoring and accountability on behalf of the whole Church (11). It encouraged each College and Course to express its aims in relation to the Ordinal of the Book of Common Prayer and the Alternative Service Book (12).

III. THE IMPACT OF NEW PROCEDURES, INTRODUCED AFTER ACCM PAPER NO.22

New procedures for theological training have been implemented in all the theological Colleges and Courses over the last five years. Revised assessment procedures have formed an integral part of a major change in the training of candidates for ordained and nationally accredited lay ministry. This change is now outlined under three headings:

A) Devolution and Accountability

The procedures established under ACCM Paper No.22 have devolved immediate responsibility for the training of ordinands to the Colleges and Courses. This responsibility is held within a partnership with the whole Church, represented by the House of Bishops and the Advisory Board of Ministry. In addition there are other forms of accountability such as that to individual bishops, to governing bodies, dioceses and parishes which receive clergy trained in the Colleges and Courses. Three particular forms of accountability are:

i) A response to ACCM Paper No.22, given every five years. This outlines the content, methods and assessment procedures used in each College or Course and relates them to the aims of ministerial training (13). The response from the College or Course is considered in depth through a visit from members of the ABM Committee concerned with the validation of ministerial training. The Committee has members nominated from amongst the Colleges and Courses, together with members chosen for their educational and theological expertise.

As the responses from Colleges and Courses have been received, the ABM has taken the opportunity to review and reflect on these developments. (This work is outlined in section IV below.) This analysis and evaluation has been fed back to Colleges and Courses so that ministerial training can continue to develop throughout the five-year validation period. Each College and Course is thus enabled to gain from some awareness of the overall pattern of training across all the Colleges and Courses. On the basis of this validation and monitoring, the ABM is able to advise the House of Bishops whether it considers that a College or Course offers courses appropriate for the training of ordinands. Candidates following a course approved in this way can be assisted from central Church funds (the Central Fund for Ministerial Training).

ii) Much depends on the effective delivery of the plans and proposals contained in each College or Course response. ABM appoints an External Examiner for each theological College and Course to monitor the effectiveness of the educational programme and forms of student assessment. The primary task of the External Examiner is one of "moderation" to ensure that the training provided meets the objectives which have been established by the College or Course. The External Examiners provide annual reports to the ABM and to the College or Course, and also meet annually together as a Board.

The ABM, together with the Colleges and Courses, also seeks to promote staff in-service training and curriculum development.

iii) The House of Bishops appoints Bishops' Inspectors. These Inspectors are independent of the validation and monitoring provided by the ABM. They exercise an oversight on behalf of the wider Church by means of a confidential report direct to the House of Bishops which goes also to the College or Course. The Bishops' Inspectors have the opportunity, through an intensive five-yearly visit or visits to a College or Course, to assess an institution both for its theological training and its guidance to students in their preparation for ordination. The

Inspectors advise the House of Bishops as they decide whether a College or Course should continue to have formal recognition for ordination training in the Church of England. Educational advice given by the Bishops' Inspectors is subsequently referred to the ABM.

B) The College or Course Responses to Three Questions

Under the review of ministerial training initiated by ACCM Paper No.22, each College or Course has been asked to provide a substantial document which responds to three primary questions:

i) *What Ordained Ministry Does the Church of England Require?*

Responses are intended to provide a theological basis for ministerial training. They are to relate this to God's presence and action in the world and in the Church, as Creator and Saviour; to give attention to the Church's mission as well as its ministry; and to explore the relation between ordained ministry and lay ministry.

ii) *What is the Shape of the Educational Programme Best Suited for Equipping People to Exercise this Ministry?*

Responses are intended to show a clear set of objectives for training. They must include a rationale for the educational programme, as well as a clear plan for each part of the programme.

iii) *What are the Appropriate Means of Assessing Suitability for the Exercise of this Ministry?*

Responses must provide a plan for assessment which will gauge whether individual students have met the objectives outlined in response to the second question. There is encouragement to adopt a variety of means of assessment (14).

ACCM Paper No.22 itself provided a sample discussion of each of the three questions (15).

C) **Priorities and Emphases in Theological Training**

The work undertaken in response to ACCM Paper No.22 has encouraged a number of shifts in theological education over the last five years, illustrated by the following six points.

i) Programmes of theological education are giving increasing emphasis to the *mission* of the Church as God's mission in the world, and are less dominated by concern with ministry in terms of maintenance and pastoral care (16).

ii) There is increasing emphasis on training which can equip ordinands to *communicate* their knowledge and understanding to others. This has in view the preparation of ordinands to participate in mission and evangelism (17).

iii) Greater emphasis is now given to preparation for a ministry which is to be carried out in *collaboration* with others. The particular purposes of ordained ministry are to be understood in the context of the corporate ministry of the whole Church (18).

iv) Responses to the first question in ACCM Paper No.22 have led Colleges and Courses to articulate a clearer theological basis for the training they offer. This has helped to clarify the purposes of ordained ministry for all concerned (19).

v) Greater clarity about the aims of ordination training has helped Colleges and Courses to be more precise about the coordination of various elements in training. It is possible to see how the parts of the curriculum, the teaching methods and the forms of assessment, are a working out of the aims and objectives. The criteria by which students are assessed now give more weight to the development of ministerial skills such as the capacity to collaborate, or act as agents of change. Emphasis can also be given to the students' growth in prayer and spiritual life (20). This has also helped to clarify ways in which the staff of Colleges and Courses can be assisted in their own development as theological teachers and educators so that they can provide the forms of training now required.

vi) If theological education is to serve the task of God's mission, it will need to be conceived as a *life-long* process of personal and corporate development. Training provided in Colleges and Courses can only serve as the *initial* stage in which the fundamental pattern is set (21). The ABM together with the House of Bishops, has sought to promote a system of "profiling" to record the development of ordinands during their initial training so that there can be greater continuity between initial, post-ordination and continuing ministerial education in the Church of England (22).

IV. ASSESSMENT OF THE RESPONSES BY COLLEGES AND COURSES

The ABM has now prepared two reports which analyse developments in theological training since the implementation of ACCM Paper No.22. Both reports are intended to foster theological and educational discussion, and neither offer final or systematic statements. The reports are available to those concerned with questions of ministry and education in dioceses as well as in other Churches.

The first Report, *Ordination and the Church's Ministry*, was published in 1991 as ABM Ministry Paper No.1. This Report, prepared under the Chairmanship of Canon Professor Rowan Williams, provides an interim evaluation of the College and Course responses to the first question posed in ACCM Paper No.22: "What ordained ministry does the Church of England require?". It emphasises the significant fact that so many responses from Colleges and Courses are grounded in an understanding of the Trinity (23).

A second Report, *Integration and Assessment*, was concerned with Educational Practice, completed in 1991. This Report, prepared under the Chairmanship of the Revd Canon Dr Sehon Goodridge (Principal of the Simon of Cyrene Theological Institute) provides an interim evaluation of the College and Course responses to the second and third questions in ACCM Paper No.22 "What is the shape of the educational programme best suited to equipping people to exercise this ministry", and "What are the appropriate means of assessing suitability for the exercise of this ministry". The Report has been published as ABM Ministry Paper No.3.

This Report provides advice on various methods for making links in the educational programme and forms of assessment for students. Examples of good practice are explored. The part which placements in parishes and secular institutions can play as an integral element in the educational programme is also considered (24). Attention is given to how ordinands can be assisted to learn from their previous and current experience of the Church, of secular life and work, through well-planned educational opportunities (25).

Colleges and Courses are being encouraged to establish a continuing process of review and development. This includes regular course evaluation, with analysis of student responses and staff judgements. Colleges and Courses should also consider the experience of those who have recently been ordained, as well as seek feedback from clergy and parishes which have received these ordinands (26).

The second Report gives some consideration to the contribution which Universities and Colleges of Higher Education might make to theological training in the rapidly changing circumstances of the 1990s. It is now the case that all theological Colleges have a link with either a University or CNAA for validation. With the demise of CNAA, future alternative forms of validation are being explored. Some theological Courses have or are exploring external validation through a University Department or College of Higher Education.

A number of Bachelor of Theology degrees, which allow scope for bringing together theory and practice within an overall programme of ministerial training, have existed for some years and these are currently being developed further in the light of ACCM Paper No.22. Similar new degrees have recently been agreed and introduced by a number of Universities. There is an encouraging trend for the Universities to be responsive to the needs which the Church has in the training of its ministers.

V. CONCLUSION

ACCM Paper No.22 has formed the basis for a thorough restructuring of theological education in the Church of England. The restructuring has been theologically based and practically oriented. Colleges and Courses have a much greater responsibility for working out in detail the aim, content, integration and assessment of their courses. They remain accountable to the Bishops' Inspectors and to ABM. ABM, in particular, seeks to aid them in the development of their educational programming through the work of the External Examiners and Working Parties such as those which produced the Reports *Ordination and the Church's Ministry* and *Integration and Assessment*. As the process moves into its second five-year period it is clear that strong foundations have been laid in the initial responses to those questions that were put, and continuing development may confidently be expected.

July 1992

The Revd Dr Nicholas Sagovsky
Chairman, IMEC

Notes:

(1) *Residence - An Education*, ACCM Occasional Paper No.38, November, 1990, p.10, and *Ordination Training on Courses*, ACCM Occasional Paper No.30, February, 1989, pp.25-6.

(2) *Deacons Now, the Report of a Church of England Working Party concerned with Women in Ordained Ministry*, ACCM, 1991, pp.24-5.

(3) *Deacons Now*, page 27.

(4) Mark Hodge, *Patterns of Ministerial Training in the Theological Colleges and Courses*, ACCM, 1988, p.8 and Chapter 5.

(5) *Residence - An Education*, Chapter 9, and *Deacons Now*, Chapter 5.

(6) Mark Hodge, *Non-Stipendiary Ministry in the Church of England*, 1983; Peter Baelz and William Jacob, Editors, *Ministers of the Kingdom, Exploration in Non-Stipendiary Ministry*, CIO, 1985; and *Regulations for Non-Stipendiary Ministry*, ACCM Occasional Paper No.23, March, 1987.

(7) *Local NSM, the Report of a Church of England Working Party concerned with Local Non-Stipendiary Ministry*, ABM Policy Paper No.1, April, 1991, page 38.

(8) *Deacons Now*, pp.25-7, 33-5.

(9) *Education for the Church's Ministry: The Report of the Working Party on Assessment*, ACCM Occasional Paper No.22, January, 1987, pp.15-17 and pp.60-1.

(10) *Education for the Church's Ministry*, pp.17-21, and 61.

(11) *Education for the Church's Ministry*, page 17 and pp.62-4.

(12) *Integration and Assessment, an Interim Evaluation of College and Course Responses to ACCM Paper No.22, the Report of an ABM Working Party on Education Practice*, 1991, page 78.

(13) *Education for the Church's Ministry*, page 62.

(14) *Integration and Assessment*, pp.1-2 and pp.7-8.

(15) *Integration and Assessment*, page 78.

(16) *Education for the Church's Ministry*, page 27; *Ordination and the Church's Ministry, an Interim Evaluation of College and Course Responses to ACCM Paper No.2,* ABM Ministry Paper No.1, April, 1991, pp.9-11; and *Integration and Assessment*, pp.10-11, page 24 and pp.47-8.

(17) *Education for the Church's Ministry*, pp.39-40; and *Integration and Assessment*, page 68.

(18) *Education for the Church's Ministry*, pp.28-31; *Ordination and the Church's Ministry*, page 19, pp.26-31; *Integration and Assessment*, page 66.

(19) *Ordination and the Church's Ministry*, pages 8 and 27.

(20) *Integration and Assessment*, pp.13-14, 27-28, 35, and 64-8.

(21) *Education for the Church's Ministry*, page 34.

(22) *Integration and Assessment*, pp.71-3.

(23) *Ordination and the Church's Ministry*, pp.3-4.

(24) *Integration and Assessment*, pp.21-25.

(25) *Integration and Assessment*, pp.55-8.

(26) *Integration and Assessment*, pp.62-3.

APPENDIX B

Extract from ACCM Occasional Paper No.30

SUMMARY OF RECOMMENDATIONS of the Report of the Working Party on the Structure and Finance of Theological Courses

Educational Factors affecting Future Provision

1. That all ordination candidates living in England should have access to a high quality of training non-residentially for the ordained ministry (paragraph 38).

2. That all Courses should provide each year:

   i) a summer school of at least eight working days of study;

   ii) a minimum of six weekends, lasting from Friday suppertime until Sunday lunchtime;

   and that there should be, in addition, at least 60 hours of tutorial contact time per year spread over at least 30 evenings (paragraph 43).

3. That each student's training should include a Pastoral Studies Unit, and also a placement or placements which are equivalent in total to a 4-8 week period. That the placement should be undertaken elsewhere than in the student's home parish or, in the case of work-focused NSMs, the workplace (paragraph 45).

4. That each student should have regular meetings with a "pastoral" or "personal" tutor or chaplain, to review personal and ministerial development as well as spiritual formation (paragraph 45).

5. That there should also be one-to-one meetings between students and the core staff responsible for writing reports on them (paragraph 45).

6. That there should be no structural impediments to ordination candidates receiving an adequate training geared to the task of professional ministry (paragraph 52).

7. That specific parts of the training, should allow for the ordination candidates to be prepared for the various roles which they will undertake in public ministry (paragraph 53).

8. That year groups should have distinct courses of training throughout the year, even though they may have some joint sessions during the residential periods (paragraph 54).

9. That the lowest viability level for a Course, on educational grounds, lies between 24 and 30 ordination candidates (paragraph 57).

10. That Courses should only be asked to accept candidates for shortened courses of study in very exceptional circumstances (paragraph 59).

11. That prospective ordination candidates should not join a Course prior to selection (paragraph 60).

12. That the Principal should do a substantial amount of teaching on the Course and be available for all residential periods (paragraph 62).

13. That each Course should have a minimum of one full-time and one half-time member of core staff and that the Principal should be full-time (paragraph 63).

14. That guidelines for the core staff of any Course with more than 30 candidates should be the subject of negotiation with the Courses and Examinations Sub-Committee when validating the syllabus and curriculum under the new assessment procedure. That the ultimate decision as to the number of core staff should be made by ACCM Finance Committee (paragraph 65).

15. That the Principal should be appointed and employed by the Governing Body (paragraph 64).

16. That ancillary staff should be fully integrated into the life and organisation of the Course (paragraph 66).

17. That Courses should make strenuous efforts to comply with the guidelines for Colleges and Courses training women (paragraphs 68 and 69).

18. That Courses should be encouraged to employ an appropriate level of administrative staff (paragraph 71).

19. That the ultimate decision whether any additional administrative staff over and above the minimum level proposed in paragraph 71 may be funded centrally should be made by the ACCM Finance Committee.

20. That the Lichfield Scale should be adopted as the standard level of remuneration for the salaried core staff of Courses (paragraph 72).

21. That all salaried members of core staff should be employed directly by the Course (paragraph 73).

22. That all members of core staff must be available to teach on weekends and at Summer School (paragraph 73).

23. That the current method of recompensing ancillary staff should continue (paragraph 74).

Future Structure

24. That each Course should have a clearly defined catchment area and the assurance that, other than in exceptional circumstances, all candidates for non-residential training from the area will be expected by their sponsoring Bishops to train on the local Course (paragraph 81).

25. That no Course for non-residential ordination training should be sponsored by only one Diocese (paragraph 82).

26. That a national structure of 10-11 Courses for non-residential ordination training should be established, based on grouping of Dioceses, each endorsing one or more Courses (paragraphs 82 and 85).

27. That each endorsing Diocese should be represented on the Council of each Course it endorses (paragraph 83).

28. That the educational model to be adopted by each Course in the national structure should be agreed as part of the new assessment procedure by CESC (paragraph 87).

Control and Management

29. That each Course should have, as its Governing Body, a Council with membership including not only representatives of the endorsing Dioceses, but also persons appointed for their managerial, financial and educational expertise (paragraph 93).

30. That each Course Council should elect its own Chairman, who should not be a Sponsoring Bishop or Diocesan Director of Ordinands (paragraph 93).

31. That the remit of the Course Council should include the items listed in paragraph 95.

32. That the Council should meet each term and appoint a small Management Committee which should meet more frequently (paragraph 94).

33. That the Chairman of the Council should be Chairman of the Management Committee (paragraph 94).

34. That the remit of the Management Committee should include the items listed in paragraph 96.

35. That the Council should appoint a Board of Studies (paragraph 95).

36. That the remit of the Board of Studies should include the items listed in paragraph 97.

37. That the Principal should be responsible for the day-to-day running of the Course and for admissions/withdrawals of candidates (paragraph 98).

Financial Security

38. That the costs of Courses should be classified between fixed and variable as shown in Appendix J (paragraph 106).

39. That Courses should be required to obtain certification from ACCM that they meet the recommendations in this report as to minimum educational criteria, staffing levels and management structure (paragraph 108).

40. That, for as long as its certification remained valid, a Course should be given a rolling three-year financial undertaking that its agreed fixed costs would be met by a block grant paid termly from the Central Fund for Ordination Training (paragraph 108).

41. That variable costs per sponsored student should be met by directly-paid grants related to the number of students actually in training, subject to assessment of student need in the usual way (paragraph 108).

42. That the level of fixed and variable costs for each Course should be agreed by ACCM Finance Committee annually (paragraph 108).

43. That, for the purpose of students claiming LEA awards or of charging private students and those from other denominations, a tuition fee and maintenance fee should be calculated as set out in paras. 109 and 110.

44. That the CFMT should be credited with the value of LEA grants awarded to sponsored students and of tuition fees paid by "other" students (paragraph 111).

45. That, in monitoring the cost of training on Courses, ACCM Finance Committee should take into account the value of direct and hidden subsidies and advise the Joint Budget Committee of the extent to which the full cost of training is being met from the General Synod's Training Budget (paragraph 113).

46. That, in comparing the financial performance of the Courses, the Finance Committee should have regard to student travel costs (paragraph 114).

47. That the Theological Colleges Reserve should be re-named the "Theological Colleges and Courses Reserve" (paragraph 115).

48. That where Courses need to buy houses for their staff use should be made of the equity-sharing loan scheme provided by the Church Commissioners (paragraph 118).

49. That, if a Course finds it necessary to provide a housing allowance, the figure provided annually by the Central Stipends Authority as to

the value of a clergyman's "free" accommodation should be used as a yardstick (paragraph 118).

Implementation

50. That the House of Bishops should resolve that, in future, Courses will only be recognised for ordination training if:

    a) their syllabus and curriculum have been validated by CESC under the new assessment procedures (ACCM Occasional Paper No.22);

    and

    b) ACCM has certified that their educational criteria, staffing levels and management structure meet the minimum requirements recommended in this report (paragraph 126).

51.* That the House of Bishops should announce that, in 3 years' time, the recognition of all existing non-residential Courses will lapse (paragraph 126).

52. That the House of Bishops should ask ACCM to set up a Steering Group to assist groups of Dioceses to establish new organisations which will meet the requirements of this report (paragraph 128).

53. That each Diocesan Bishop should nominate a Diocesan official to liaise with the Steering Group (paragraph 129).

54. That consultation on these recommendations should be carried out with the Methodist and United Reformed Churches (paragraph 130).

* **Note:** *This recommendation was not supported by ACCM Council which thought it more appropriate to put forward a timetable for implementation ie. that negotiation and agreement of the new arrangements should be concluded by 31st August, 1992, and that all should be implemented before the end of a further two-year period. This ACCM proposal was endorsed by the House of Bishops.*

Part-time Theological Courses: Student Numbers 1982-1991

This table summarises the number of sponsored candidates in training. An analysis of **all** students training on part-time Theological Courses is given on the pages that follow.

Course	Sponsored Candidates in Training*									
	1982	**1983**	**1984**	**1985**	**1986**	**1987**	**1988**	**1989**	**1990**	**1991**
Canterbury	20	18	21	16	17	20	23	23	17	16
Carlisle	5	4	7	8	7	12	15	13	11	8
E. Anglia	23	20	19	20	25	26	23	25	26	26
E Midlands	17	42	30	28	31	29	21	18	14	19
Gloucester	16	12	6	22	25	17	11	10	13	14
NEOC	26	26	22	26	21	17	20	29	25	25
NOC	58	64	65	63	59	53	50	52	56	53
Oak Hill	21	20	19	20	22	25	21	26	22	29
Oxford	21	20	20	23	21	20	22	26	31	32
St Albans	11	15	12	7	8	5	3	3	4	6
SDMTS	68	59	62	59	60	54	68	72	68	70
Southwark	42	41	50	51	52	52	49	50	42	37
S.West	13	21	20	17	18	14	10	11	5	13
W.Midlands	25	25	27	19	28	26	40	43	34	26
	366	**387**	**380**	**379**	**394**	**370**	**376**	**401**	**368**	**374**

* *The figures show candidates sponsored by English Bishops and training on part-time Theological Courses in October of each year.*

Part-time Theological Courses
STUDENT NUMBERS
1982-1991

Year	Men*			Women**			Sponsored Students(CofE)			Other	++	Total	Total
(Oct)	STI+	NSM	Total	STI	NSM	Total	STI	NSM	Total	Churches	Other	Other	
Canterbury School of Ministry													
1982			13			7			20			2	22
1983			11			7			18			1	19
1984	6	9	15	2	4	6	8	13	21			-	21
1985	5	8	13	1	2	3	6	10	16			2	18
1986	5	8	13	1	3	4	6	11	17			3	20
1987	4	8	12	2	6	8	6	14	20			2	22
1988	3	8	11	3	9	12	6	17	23			-	23
1989	1	5	6	3	14	17	4	19	23			-	23
1990	2	3	5	2	10	12	4	13	17	2	-	2	19
1991	3	6	9	2	5	7	5	11	16			2	18
Carlisle Diocesan Training Institute													
1982			4			1			5			-	5
1983			3			1			4			10	14
1984	-	5	5	-	2	2	-	7	7			7	14
1985	1	5	6	-	2	2	1	7	8			7	15
1986	-	6	6	-	1	1	-	7	7			7	14
1987	1	9	10	1	1	2	2	10	12	-	6	6	18
1988	1	9	10	1	4	5	2	13	15	-	3	3	18
1989	2	5	7	1	5	6	3	10	13	1	3	4	17
1990	1	5	6	-	5	5	1	10	11	2	-	2	13
1991	-	2	2	-	6	6	-	8	8	1	3	4	12

Year (Oct)	Men* STI+	Men* NSM	Men* Total	Women** STI	Women** NSM	Women** Total	Sponsored Students(CofE) STI	Sponsored Students(CofE) NSM	Sponsored Students(CofE) Total	Other Churches	++ Other	Total Other	Total
East Anglian Ministerial Training Course													
1982			16			7			23			4	27
1983			12			8			20			4	24
1984	-	14	14	1	4	5	1	18	19			2	21
1985	1	13	14	-	6	6	1	19	20			1	21
1986	1	16	17	-	8	8	1	24	25			1	26
1987	2	15	17	1	8	9	3	23	26			-	26
1988	2	15	17	-	6	6	2	21	23			-	23
1989	2	13	15	2	8	10	4	21	25			-	25
1990	5	9	14	1	11	12	6	20	26			-	26
1991	4	8	12	3	11	14	7	19	26			-	26
East Midlands Ministry Training Course													
1982			11			6			17			33	50
1983			24			18			42			31	73
1984	1	22	23	1	6	7	2	28	30			38	68
1985	3	13	16	1	11	12	4	24	28			43	71
1986	4	16	20	3	8	11	7	24	31			36	67
1987	4	12	16	6	7	13	10	19	29	6	36	42	71
1988	2	8	10	5	6	11	7	14	21	9	36	45	66
1989	2	4	6	9	3	12	11	7	18	8	40	48	66
1990	1	3	4	4	6	10	5	9	14	10	45	55	69
1991	1	8	9	4	6	10	5	14	19	10	45	55	74

Year (Oct)	Men* STI+	Men* NSM	Men* Total	Women** STI	Women** NSM	Women** Total	Sponsored Students(CofE) STI	Sponsored Students(CofE) NSM	Sponsored Students(CofE) Total	Other Churches	++ Other	Total Other	Total
Gloucester School of Ministry													
1982			11			5			16			26	42
1983			10			2			12			32	44
1984	1	4	5	-	1	1	1	5	6			53	59
1985	4	14	18	1	3	4	5	17	22			42	64
1986	1	19	20	1	4	5	2	23	25			29	54
1987	3	9	12	-	5	5	3	14	17	-	35	35	52
1988	2	3	5	-	6	6	2	9	11	-	23	23	34
1989	-	3	3	2	5	7	2	8	10	-	28	28	38
1990	-	7	7	3	3	6	3	10	13	-	43	43	56
1991	1	8	9	3	2	5	4	10	14	1	26	27	41
North East Ordination Course													
1982			20			6			26			2	28
1983			19			7			26			3	29
1984	2	11	13	3	6	9	5	17	22			2	24
1985	3	11	14	6	6	12	9	17	26			2	28
1986	2	7	9	5	7	12	7	14	21			5	26
1987	-	8	8	6	3	9	6	11	17	1	1	2	19
1988	4	6	10	5	5	10	9	11	20	2	-	2	22
1989	7	9	16	4	9	13	11	18	29	1	-	1	30
1990	5	6	11	3	11	14	8	17	25	3	1	4	29
1991	3	6	9	3	13	16	6	19	25	3	1	4	29

Year (Oct)	Men* STI+	Men* NSM	Men* Total	Women** STI	Women** NSM	Women** Total	Sponsored Students(CofE) STI	Sponsored Students(CofE) NSM	Sponsored Students(CofE) Total	Other Churches	++ Other	Total Other	Total
Northern Ordination Course													
1982			46			12			58			3	61
1983			49			15			64			4	68
1984	22	28	50	4	11	15	26	39	65			2	67
1985	20	24	44	5	14	19	25	38	63			2	65
1986	18	22	40	8	11	19	26	33	59			6	65
1987	14	20	34	9	10	19	23	30	53	6	3	9	62
1988	16	17	33	8	9	17	24	26	50	10	-	10	60
1989	16	17	33	8	11	19	24	28	52	8	2	10	62
1990	18	15	33	11	12	23	29	27	56	12	-	12	68
1991	15	18	33	13	7	20	28	25	53	13	1	14	67
Oak Hill Ministerial Training Course													
1982			19			2			21			2	23
1983			16			4			20			-	20
1984	-	12	12	-	7	7	-	19	19			2	21
1985	-	12	12	1	7	8	1	19	20			9	29
1986	-	13	13	2	7	9	2	20	22			6	28
1987	-	12	12	4	9	13	4	21	25	6	4	10	35
1988	-	9	9	3	9	12	3	18	21	2	1	3	24
1989	1	11	12	4	10	14	5	21	26	2	1	3	29
1990	2	14	16	1	5	6	3	19	22	2	-	2	24
1991	1	20	21	-	8	8	1	28	29	3	8	11	40

Year (Oct)	Men* STI+	Men* NSM	Men* Total	Women** STI	Women** NSM	Women** Total	Sponsored Students(CofE) STI	Sponsored Students(CofE) NSM	Sponsored Students(CofE) Total	Other Churches	++ Other	Total Other	Total
Oxford Ministry Course													
1982			21			-			21			6	27
1983			20			-			20			3	23
1984	-	19	19	-	1	1	-	20	20			4	24
1985	-	21	21	-	2	2	-	23	23			3	26
1986	-	16	16	-	5	5	-	21	21			4	25
1987	1	14	15	-	5	5	1	19	20	-	2	2	22
1988	-	16	16	-	6	6	-	22	22	-	1	1	23
1989	2	14	16	-	10	10	2	24	26	-	2	2	28
1990	-	12	12	3	16	19	3	28	31	-	-	-	31
1991	1	15	16	3	13	16	4	28	32	-	-	-	32
St Albans Diocese Ministerial Training Scheme													
1982			7			4			11			50	61
1983			6			9			15			53	68
1984	1	4	5	4	3	7	5	7	12			53	65
1985	2	1	3	2	2	4	4	3	7			48	55
1986	1	3	4	2	2	4	3	5	8			46	54
1987	1	1	2	2	1	3	3	2	5	4	42	46	51
1988	1	1	2	-	1	1	1	2	3	4	49	53	56
1989	-	3	3	-	-	-	-	3	3	5	50	55	58
1990	-	2	2	-	2	2	-	4	4	3	55	58	62
1991	-	2	2	2	2	4	2	4	6	4	46	50	56

Year (Oct)	Men* STI+	Men* NSM	Men* Total	Women** STI	Women** NSM	Women** Total	Sponsored Students(CofE) STI	Sponsored Students(CofE) NSM	Sponsored Students(CofE) Total	Other Churches	++ Other	Total Other	Total
Southern Dioceses Ministerial Training Scheme													
1982			52			16			68			5	73
1983			38			21			59			4	63
1984	4	36	40	3	19	22	7	55	62			2	64
1985	5	29	34	7	18	25	12	47	59			5	64
1986	3	30	33	6	21	27	9	51	60			8	68
1987	3	28	31	4	19	23	7	47	54	9	3	12	66
1988	3	35	38	3	27	30	6	62	68	6	-	6	74
1989	4	35	39	5	28	33	9	63	72	7	-	7	79
1990	3	27	30	7	31	38	10	58	68	15	-	15	83
1991	6	30	36	7	27	34	13	57	70	20	-	20	90
Southwark Ordination Course													
1982			31			11			42			12	54
1983			40			1			41			12	53
1984	10	27	37	5	8	13	15	35	50			8	58
1985	6	28	34	6	11	17	12	39	51			-	51
1986	11	27	38	4	10	14	15	37	52			11	63
1987	10	24	34	4	14	18	14	38	52	6	2	8	60
1988	7	22	29	8	12	20	15	34	49	6	2	8	57
1989	3	18	21	10	19	29	13	37	50	6	2	8	58
1990	3	16	19	7	16	23	10	32	42	6	2	8	50
1991	3	12	15	7	15	22	10	27	37	9	1	10	47

Year (Oct)	Men* STI+	Men* NSM	Men* Total	Women** STI	Women** NSM	Women** Total	Sponsored Students(CofE) STI	Sponsored Students(CofE) NSM	Sponsored Students(CofE) Total	Other Churches	++ Other	Total Other	Total
South-West Ministry Training Course													
1982			10			3			13			12	25
1983			16			5			21			2	23
1984	3	12	15	-	5	5	3	17	20			10	30
1985	1	8	9	1	7	8	2	15	17			9	26
1986	1	8	9	2	7	9	3	15	18			4	22
1987	1	6	7	2	5	7	3	11	14	1	3	4	18
1988	-	5	5	1	4	5	1	9	10	2	3	5	15
1989	2	5	7	1	3	4	3	8	11	5	2	7	18
1990	1	4	5	-	-	-	1	4	5	7	-	7	12
1991	3	6	9	3	1	4	6	7	13	8	1	9	22
West Midlands Ministerial Training Course													
1982			13			12			25			11	36
1983			11			14			25			6	31
1984	-	9	9	-	18	18	-	27	27			4	31
1985	-	1	1	5	13	18	5	14	19			3	22
1986	1	5	6	12	10	22	13	15	28			16	44
1987	4	6	10	7	9	16	11	15	26	8	15	23	49
1988	6	13	19	10	11	21	16	24	40	7	6	13	53
1989	8	11	19	11	13	24	19	24	43	9	2	11	54
1990	2	9	11	10	13	23	12	22	34	11	6	17	51
1991	3	6	9	6	11	17	9	17	26	12	3	15	41

* *These figures are those training for ordination to the priesthood.*

** *These figures include a few men and women training to be accredited layworkers. From 1987, the figures include those women training for ordination to the diaconate.*

\+ *Separate figures of those training for stipendiary and non-stipendiary ministry are not available before 1984.*

\+ + *These figures include those in training who were: already ordained, intending to come forward for selection, candidates from other Provinces and lay students. Separate figures for candidates from other Churches are not available prior to 1987.*

SPONSORED CANDIDATES RECOMMENDED FOR TRAINING

	STIPENDIARY			NON-STIPENDIARY			ALL
	Priests	**Other***	**Total**	**Priests**	**Other***	**Total**	
1982	350	60	410	110	45	155	565
1983	303	61	364	87	41	128	492
1984	306	68	374	92	49	141	515
1985	347	80	427	83	51	134	561
1986	363	87	450	84	49	133	583
1987	320	81	401	73	53	126	527
1988	252	81	333	50	55	105	438
1989	239	69	308	63	68	131	439
1990	264	71	335	48	55	103	438
1991	274	86	360	51	39	90	450

* *"Other" includes candidates recommended to train for Deaconess, Deacon and Accredited Lay Worker.*

APPENDIX E

MINIMUM LEVEL OF STAFFING FOR A THEOLOGICAL COLLEGE

Extract from the Minutes of the ACCM Committee for Theological Education: 2nd and 3rd July 1990

The Bishops' Committee on Inspections had requested advice from CTE concerning the minimum level of staffing for a Theological College. CTE's comments and their implications would be reported to the House of Bishops in due course.

The Committee noted that a staff:student ratio of 1:10 is currently in use in assessing the staffing level for Theological Colleges. It was reported that this was the ratio for civic universities in the 1960's and historically this had provided the educational benchmark for the ratio. Since this time Universities have moved to a less favourable ratio, up towards 1:15, on financial grounds. Information received from a Polytechnic and a College of Higher Education indicated that as regards theology a staff:student ratio in such institutions would now be approximately 1:15. However, the Committee considered that the current ratio of 1:10 was justifiable given the unique role of Theological Colleges and Courses in providing ministerial formation and spirituality compared to the universities and other forms of education. This makes for a significant difference regarding vocational and professional development which could justify 1:10 as an appropriate ratio.

It was also realised that there are main subjects which, however integrated, need to be taught and learned in a Theological College. The Committee envisaged as appropriate a minimum of five posts for a Theological College, given that one or more of the posts might be divided into part-time appointments. This may be necessary as there could be more than five areas of expertise required, such as Old Testament, New Testament, Doctrine, Worship, Pastoral Studies and Ethics. The concern was also expressed that Church History may not always be adequately covered unless it is an area of expertise for at least a part-time member of staff.

The Committee also underlined the importance of having in each Theological College a body of colleagues who can debate amongst themselves theological and educational issues. Lively engagement of this kind is essential to undergird theological learning and also to assist in linking theological subjects with mission, spirituality, pastoral formation and to serve the need for integration. It was considered that five posts could provide the basis for such engagement, and that thought might be given to how best administrative help could be provided to free theological teachers from some of the administrative responsibilities in order to allow them to concentrate on their primary tasks.

It was agreed that these comments could form the response to the Bishops' Committee on Inspections.

APPENDIX F

BASIC EDUCATIONAL AND FINANCIAL FACTORS RELEVANT TO INSTITUTIONS PROVIDING FULL-TIME ORDINATION TRAINING

(Note: The importance of these factors was endorsed by the House of Bishops in January 1991)

A. EDUCATIONAL FACTORS TO CONSIDER

Realistic expectations of future recruitment.

Possibility of achieving desirable size factors for:

- student year groups (to allow viable courses for 3-year degrees, 3-year certificates and 2-year certificates).
- establishing an ethos of ordination training (satisfactory balance with any other training carried on in the College).
- number of staff to teach the range of subjects (unless certain skills are available locally) and to formulate syllabus/curriculum.
- number of staff to provide a variety of viewpoints and to illustrate teamwork.
- number of staff to provide a body of colleagues who can debate amongst themselves theological and education issues. (The Committee for Theological Education believes that five posts is the minimum for such engagement.)

Possibility of maintaining 1:10 staff:student ratio.

The presence in the locality of a good opportunity for interaction and cooperation with some or all of the following:

- the Theological Courses.
- University Departments of Theology and Religious Studies.
- the Colleges of other denominations.
- Church Colleges of Higher Education.

B. FINANCIAL FACTORS TO CONSIDER

Present and anticipated future costs and fee levels and costs (at current prices) on the assumption that the College can recruit the full Bishops' Allocation, with a view to maintaining those Colleges which are expected to be the most economical to operate in the medium term.

Overall financial resources of College including:

- availability of capital funds and willingness of trustees to subsidise training and to undertake to continue to do so.
- need to raise funds to finance existing buildings (eg. new buildings constructed with borrowed funds) reflected by a deficit on net working capital in College balance sheet.
- existence of short-term financing problems, reflected by net current liabilities in the College balance sheet.
- opportunities to develop income from conferences.
- opportunities for development of the College as an educational resource for the Church.

Age and quality of buildings including:

- adequacy of property for academic purposes.
- availability of suitable accommodation for single and married ordinands at an economic cost.
- adequacy and economy of staff housing.
- probability of major costs arising in next ten to twenty years on items such as re-roofing, rewiring, new heating systems, replumbing.

Ability of College to recruit additional students from other sources, eg. non-ordinands, the Anglican Communion, other denominations, taking into account the impact of such a change in balance on the ethos of the training provided.

(*Note*: Some Colleges fill spare rooms with lodgers studying in other institutions. Although this brings in income towards maintenance overhead costs, it makes no contribution towards the cost of teaching in a College.)

APPENDIX G

PAPER FROM THE PRINCIPALS OF THE THEOLOGICAL COLLEGES

Present Problems in Full-Time Theological Education and a Strategy for the Future

A contribution to the current debate from the Principals of the Theological Colleges, who had a full-day meeting at Church House on 21st October, 1991, meetings in small groups to produce drafts on specific topics in November and December, and a residential meeting for 24 hours at the Royal Foundation of St Katharine on 15th-16th January, 1992. Two Course Principals participated in all these discussions.

The document that follows is concerned both with the situation that confronts us now and with the longer view in relation to the following areas of discussion:

1. The present situation: diversity of Colleges; problems of increased cost and decrease in numbers of ordinands; need to develop a national strategy for quality in training.

2. A restatement of a rationale for a two or three-year period of full-time education in Theological College as one component of a mixed-mode approach to ministerial training.

3. The possibilities for developing Theological Colleges as resources for the training of the whole people of God, in addition to their primary purpose of preparing for ordination.

4. Possible and actual developments in the linking of resources for theological education on a regional basis.

5. The importance of training an adequate supply of theologians and teachers, both to supply staff for Colleges and Courses (and to work in Universities), and to meet the wider needs of the Church.

6. Difficulties in finance: costs of training to the Church; problems of funding for the Colleges; suggested ways forward.

Section 1 Partnership as a basic principle

We want to set this discussion in the context of the first two questions which College and Course Principals have all had to address in our responses to ACCM 22:

a) What ordained ministry does the Church of England require?

b) What is the shape of the educational programme best suited for equipping people to exercise this ministry?

We agreed it as of paramount importance that the quality of training be maintained and improved so as to give assurance of competence in professional ministry. To this end we recognise a need for a genuine and enhanced partnership between all those groups involved in preparing men and women for such ministry. We affirm the diversity of standpoint and tradition of the Colleges, but wish to see this within the contexts of partnership between us all, and the ecumenical challenge.

Another part of the context for the current discussion is given us by the Church's increasing difficulty in financing training, and by the fact that there are significantly fewer ministerial candidates in training than the Colleges can accommodate. We urge that cost of training be considered in relation to the value of the years of service subsequently given to the Church. It must be borne in mind, too, that the cost of training is only one item in the provision of ordained ministry, and must be considered alongside housing, stipend, and eventual pension.

We recognise that finance will influence, but not dictate, options for change, and that closures and mergers may have to be considered. We would urge that such closures and mergers take place only in the setting of a coherent strategy for the development of Christian training nationwide. We see this training as one whole, including the encouragement of vocation, pre-College development, the College or Course engagement, and post-ordination training. We would point out that the shortfall of ordinands is being used by some Colleges as the starting point of a deliberate policy to enrol candidates preparing for other forms of ministry, and that this participation of lay people and ordinands in training is something we affirm and would wish to see develop.

We welcome changes made in the carrying out of an evolutionary strategy. These changes do not necessarily require more money, rather an examination of how costs are shared between those who are partners in providing such training. In what follows we indicate the changes we think desirable. We would stress that training be understood as partnership if quality is to be its criterion and characteristic.

The management of resources for training in ministry involves different levels of management and accountability, all of which have the aims of financial responsibility and quality in ministry. Where these agencies act as partners, option for change can be identified and implemented. The obvious partners in management for training in ministry are, on the one hand, the House of Bishops and General Synod, together with the advisory bodies of ABM and the Committee on Inspections, added to which are the appropriate bodies in other participating Churches. On the other hand are the Colleges and Courses. Yet training for ministry requires a wider partnership: Universities, Polytechnics, social agencies and independent bodies; diocesan and non-Anglican and Anglican boards and individuals. The number of partners increases if training includes discovery of vocation and post-ordination on-the-job training, as we consider it should. Those who provide the training are as much beneficiaries of the partnership as those who receive it.

The following paragraphs deal with the development of partnerships in five important areas:

1. Partnerships in the context as well as the substance of full-time training for ministry; (Section 2)

2. Colleges and Courses, in partnership with other agencies, as resources for the whole Church; (Section 3)

3. Partnership between resources for theological training at two levels: the single larger institution in partnership with one other large institution, eg. a University; the cluster of smaller institutions working together in a variety of relationships; (Section 4)

4. Partnership with academic societies to provide for the training of theologians and participation in studies in the humanities; (Section 5)

5. Partnership in financing training so as to ensure responsible management of capital and of fixed and variable costs. (Section 6)

Section 2 Partners in training: the Colleges as training partners in the period from early vocation to post-ordination. Context and substance

Our concern as College Principals is primarily with the two to three-year period of full-time training which the Churches require for many of their ordinands. While we all affirm the value of the distinctiveness and diversity of and within our Colleges, we are all committed to seeing that training involves encounter with other traditions of Anglicanism than our own, and with other parts of the Christian Church.

Typically, several institutions and individuals are engaged in the training of an ordinand over the seven to ten years that separate the detection of early signs of vocation and the taking up of major responsibility. During the latter part of this training, the candidate is on the payroll of the Church. The cost of this training is thereby shared, and together with other costs of training must be set against the value of service in subsequent ministry. It should also be recognised that a candidate is of value to others whether teachers, fellow-learners, or providers of the context for learning in the process seen as a whole. However, the purpose of this section is to indicate the kinds of interaction that the College experience, as a two or three-year intensive engagement within the longer period, makes possible. We urge that this full-time learning experience be maintained as an important element available in training for ministry.

The years of training are life-changing as well as informational. The College, as a component in this process, provides five contexts in which change can be given impetus. Each context has its own, as well as a cumulative, value; each mirrors, in a concise way, interactions found more generally in church community. The five types of interaction required in training and found in College are:

1. The interaction with a Christian community where, successively, roles expressive of lay person and minister are tried, modified and adopted. The College is midway between parish of early formation and later ministry.

2. The one-to-one relationship of student and tutor, where fact-finding and conclusion drawing are tried and tested. The College is midway between early vocation-assessing and training incumbent/trainee-minister, which entail significant one-to-one relationships.

3. The engagement of individuals with others in collaborative effort - the pattern of future work, especially in target-centred activity.

4. The participation of individuals in a larger community, to learn about patterns of human relating and about self. By being in the larger community an individual has to come to terms with personal strengths and weaknesses in ministry. This full-time engagement, to include spouse and children, with the rhythms of term and vacation prepare for ministry as a style of life, as well as enhancing insights, skills, and knowledge which can later be exercised from this style of life.

5. The small group, where experience of leading and being led envisages a collaborative pattern of ministry.

There are, during the College years, other institutions and agencies, especially those involving wider concerns, professional standards, and ecumenical encounter. These too provide occasion and context to make possible students' experience and interaction, and make it feasible to integrate received tradition and expertise with current enterprise. Hence some assurance can be given of the quality of subsequent ministry. We recognise that the College period has value that cannot be quantified, and draw attention to the following four aspects which College life provides:

1. Sustained participation in the ongoing life of the Church's prayer, enabling present growth, but envisaging later years when initial enthusiasm has run out, the well run dry.

2. Sustained encounter with ministers, scholars, professionals, and libraries to prepare for continued and self-motivated learning and living in the very much later years.

3. The intellectual and emotional engagement with peer group or others, in order to understand previous roles and to adjust to new ones.

4. The formation of lasting friendships and support groups.

We therefore urge that present patterns of partnership between the centre and Colleges continue, in order to provide this element of in-depth College life as part of the strategy which may envisage mixed modes of training.

Section 3 Partners in resource: Colleges and Courses, with other agencies, as a resource for the Churches as a whole

The main purpose of Theological Colleges is to serve the whole Church by preparing men and women for ordained or accredited ministry. While this necessitates a withdrawal for study, prayer and reflection, there is also an intensive engagement and involvement in different contexts in Church and society. In this way preparation for ministry takes place in the setting of the whole people of God. A combination of resources is needed for these two elements, the one of withdrawal and the other of engagement. This combination of resources presents possibilities (and in many cases actualities) for a College or Course to be of service to the Churches on three levels of encounter: local, regional and national. We recognise that diversification might hinder or confuse the primary purpose of ordination training, but note that worthwhile initiatives have been made, with benefit on an international as well as on local, regional and national levels, and in ecumenical as well as Anglican settings.

We would urge, therefore, that Colleges (where appropriate) be encouraged to make resources available locally, regionally and nationally, and so be a resource on those levels at least. It is the more important, therefore, that no closure of a College or Course be envisaged which would deprive a region of such resource, unless such a loss made significant compensating gains elsewhere.

The initiatives we would wish to see encouraged are:

1. Locally, where there is interaction between students and their placements, and staff contributions.

2. Regionally, or at a diocesan level, where there is cooperation between Colleges and Courses, and an involvement with post ordination training and continuing ministerial education.

3. Nationally (and internationally) that there should be the sponsoring of conferences, programmes (eg. God on Monday Project at Ridley Hall) and ministerial or educational study schemes.

4. The further development of the principle that ordinands train with lay people and others, either through sharing the College facilities or through participation in common elements in a programme. It would be possible for a College to be a diocesan, inter-diocesan and ecumenical resource, and so provide a more constructive context for pre or post-ordination training. This development suggests both the making available of buildings as well as staff, and the making available of staff off the site.

5. Consideration should be given that one College at least might initiate, or combine in other institutions' initiatives, distance learning programmes; also that some Colleges might participate in modular schemes of training. Further developments on the model of the Open University ought to be seriously considered.

The Colleges are therefore significant contributors to training, and are already committed to diversification for the benefit of others as well as the ordained ministry. This diversification should be fostered where it enhances the following of the primary aim, and entrepreneurial activity does not detract from the purpose of ordination training. We would however point out that present staff of theological Colleges are over-stretched, and that developments such as those outlined above would themselves have to be properly resourced in terms of teaching and administrative personnel.

Section 4 Partners in resource: partnerships between Colleges and other institutions serving the region

A development of the argument in Section 3 is that Colleges have a part to play in making up a cluster of resources available in and to a region, but which would also be available more generally on a national basis. It would not be a requirement that students be directed as a matter of course to their nearest regional centre, even if that were a possible option sometimes adopted.

It must be admitted that it has taken much time and thought to achieve any clarity on the concept of "a cluster of resources serving a region", and even now it must be recognised that a clarity of vision may not lead to a strategy which is generally applicable on a national basis. Perhaps the most that can realistically be hoped for is the fostering of federal relationships where these have met a demonstrated need, together with the recognition that two types of clustering have value. First, the grouping of a number of smaller units close together, in a place on which lines of communication converge; second, the setting of a larger unit adjacent to an institution of some size, usually a University. It must be recognised that centres of excellence may begin with a regional intent, but become in time centres of national recourse. It is this as much as anything that has made it difficult to speak in simple terms of "regionalisation".

There are some regions readily identifiable where lines of communication do converge on a cluster of resources; there are some Colleges and Courses which have gone some way to partnership. Elsewhere, it is impossible to regard a region as having any definition or autonomy (for example, the North is too indeterminate and has had institutions moved away from it); or as having easily defined boundaries with its neighbours. We would not favour any re-location of a large institution to create a cluster in a new setting, but would see the rationale for a small-scale transfer of funds if strategic planning made them available*. (Some such might well be advantageous within the total resources of such a region as Manchester-Merseyside). In the fostering of federal relationships, we suggest the following factors be considered.

1. The closeness of the institutions to each other, and the speed and ease of travel to them from the hinterland: otherwise increased travel and administrative costs could offset other economies.

2. The diversity and spread within Anglicanism as well as the range of other Christian traditions; a suitable "mix" of students from the whole country would be needed to counteract the risk of provincialism.

3. The need to ensure that a large enough range of resources were available: Courses as well as College, University and/or tertiary College, ecumenical institution (Roman Catholic as well as URC and Methodist, and Baptist if possible) and also an interaction with CME and part-time or evening learning schemes.

* *One College Principal asked us to note his divergent view "I would favour the relocation of one or two of the Oxford or Cambridge Colleges, or others, to Manchester or Sheffield".*

4. The desirability of working with dioceses which are adjacent to each other, in order that diocesan schemes (vocational, lay, post-ordination) might benefit from, and contribute to, such clusters of resources.

Yet we recognise the difficulties of implementing such a strategy, whether discussion start with the identification of a cluster of resources and move on to suggest a region which they could be said to serve; or whether it begin with a notional region and consider the institutions which seem to lie at its centre and serve it. We would, however, wish to see the fostering of initiatives which have demonstrated their worth: and which could be a national as well as a regional asset.

Section 5 Partners in theology: the training of theologians

The resource which Colleges and Courses most closely partner is the University. This partnership is most effective and valuable where the University is nearby, and the University department, large, stable and well-balanced with regard to subjects and teachers. There must also be a genuine partnership and mutual confidence, resulting in a two-way discussion of the shape and nature of the University course and a recognition of the needs of the College or Course. Clearly, the department must be sufficiently secure financially for it to guarantee consistency in the shape of the degree. Polytechnics are also possible partners, whether for teaching or for validation - this last, especially because of the ending of the CNAA. But caution should be exercised if partnership in teaching with Polytechnics is envisaged, where there may be too heavy a weighting on the phenomenological rather than a theological approach to the discipline. We urge that partnership with Universities be encouraged in order to emphasise the importance of the trained mind, the value of theology for the Churches, and the due part of theology in studies in the humanities. Some of us have found that links with Colleges of Education have proved to be of great value. We consider these elements to be of prime concern to these ends:

1. The participation of College staff in the academic community - whether as teachers, or as researchers proceeding to higher degrees or publication.

2. The recognition that time for study and research is essential to the teaching staff so that the wider needs of the Churches may be met.

3. The encouragement of suitable students to undertake research, whether for a further degree or otherwise, so that there may be a supply of fit persons to teach in Colleges or Courses, to engage in ministry or teaching more widely in tertiary education, and to provide for the intellectual, pastoral and educational needs of the Churches beyond the academic arena.

4. The possibility that a College might specialise, or have a concern, in a particular discipline or theme: though not at the cost of isolating any one part of the field from the whole.

5. The recognition that a College contributes as well as derives benefit from this concern with the humanities, on both a formal and informal basis.

Section 6 Partners in accountability: central and Collegiate finance

As partners in the responsible management of capital and of fixed and variable costs we recognise also the size and acuteness of current financial problems in the Church. We are clear both that we should not simply ask for more money, and that the Church should not seek to solve immediate financial problems by short-term savings or cost-cutting measures. What is needed is the development of an overall strategy.

We have identified the following particular financial problems relating to Theological Colleges:

1. The lack of capital, and the difficulty of financing capital development. In the past, block grants by way of loan have sometimes been made available. There were also equity-sharing loans for housing. More recently many Colleges have had to rely on special appeals. While we see the place for going out to appeal for new capital (and many of us have done so recently) it is questionable whether this is the best use of our time. We also recognise that some Colleges are over-capitalised if reference is made only to the number of sponsored candidates for ordination who take up places.

2. The present system of budgeting has reduced College resources to a minimum. "Break-even" budgets, within the confines of restricted cost-of-living-index annual increase, do not allow for future

development - or for servicing or reducing loans. The 80% conference profit does not sufficiently alter the case.

3. The failure to distinguish between fixed and variable costs creates serious problems for the Colleges in budgeting, particularly in a situation where the number of students may vary substantially from year to year. Because fixed staffing costs have risen above inflation, and variable fees have been fixed in relation to inflation, unwise economies have had to be made in variable costs and necessary repairs and renewals.

4. We are not convinced that the annual fee application by each College to the London-based Finance Committee is either a good use of time or the best way of negotiating the fee. Members of the Committee may not be aware of the physical setting or limitations of each College.

The Colleges cannot continue to give good educational support to the Churches if these problems are left unresolved. The problems cannot realistically be resolved by a transfer to central management (whether by purchase or lease-back), but they can be resolved by a strategic development of the present pattern of contained independence in partnership. This partnership between the centre and the Colleges we value. We therefore suggest the following to further that partnership:

1. a) Consideration of reintroducing equity-sharing loan schemes.

   b) Where appeals are recognised as being for a necessary purpose there might be some matching grant or loan from central funds.

   c) There could be a recognised development element (eg. 10%) as an item in the annual budget.

   Any such participation in the development of a College would be seen within the Church's strategy for developing training resources beyond their primary concern of training for ordination. In this we recognise a place for entrepreneurism.

2. We would ask for the distinction between fixed and variable costs to be applied to Colleges as well as Courses. We do not believe there is any substance in the objection that block grants cannot be paid to

independent institutions, for the government funds independent Universities partly by block grants and partly by fees. For the Colleges, too, there could be a counterpart in the generation of funds (income or capital) on a local basis. We consider the distinction between fixed and variable costs a major issue in the maintenance and improvement of quality in training.

3. The present system of setting College fees, with annual discussions between the Principal and Bursar of each College and the Finance Committee could be replaced if the Finance Committee fixed a "standard" fee for all Colleges based on anticipated inflationary increases and known increases in fixed costs (eg. Lichfield Scale). Only those Colleges who wished to argue for an increase above the "standard" fee would need to appear before the Committee. A quinquennial visit from members of the Committee to the College, possibly coinciding with the Bishops' Inspectors, would ensure that detailed discussions about the finances of the College took place regularly and also that members of the Committee would gain first-hand knowledge of each different situation.

   If the distinction between fixed and variable costs were to be adopted, the "standard" fee would cover the variable element, while the fixed costs could be covered by a "block grant" for each College based on its particular circumstances and discussed in detail at each quinquennial visit.

   Annual accounts would continue to be considered by the Committee as at present.

In this way we would see finance taking its place as a consequence of planned change. There needs to be a clear partnership and a joint acceptance of responsibility between the House of Bishops, Synod, ABM and the Colleges with respect to quality as well as cost of ministry*. We wish to see the much-discussed independence of Colleges within this wider

* *One College Principal suggested the consideration that student grants be transferred to the Church Commissioners' rather than the Synod budget: the training budget being more comparable with salary costs than with other elements in the Synod budget.*

partnership. This independence is in fact already limited, not least by the financial constraints discussed above. Our view is that the cost of eliminating the limited independence that we at present have would be prohibitively high and is unnecessary, and it should remain if the Colleges are to continue as a vital resource, worthy of support, in an evolving pattern of the Churches' training.

As College Principals we welcome the chance to respond to the Advisory Group's brief, and strongly support the intention of looking at all the problems and opportunities of ministry training as a whole in the context of the whole people of God. In the past there has been, perhaps inevitably, a study of issues in isolation. Reports on finance, the Colleges, the Courses, syllabus construction and on Residence all come to mind. The fragmented approach suited to analysis has meant sometimes that discussion has not been pursued to a conclusion, and usually that an approach to the whole has not been possible. It is good that now a synthetic approach may lead to a planned overall strategy**, and that there can be an increase in confidence between the partners whose concern it is to assure a quality of ministry and responsibility in management of resources whether human or financial.

RWNH/DJL 21 February 1992

** *One College Principal who took part in the meetings has nevertheless expressed his unease with the process of discussion which led to this document: "it (the paper) does not seem to me to address, with sufficient clarity, the major issues of the independence of the Colleges, the relation between full and part-time theological education, and nor does it examine in detail the principles and practicalities involved in closures or mergers."*

APPENDIX H

Extract from letter of 21st February, 1992 from PRINCIPAL OF SALISBURY AND WELLS THEOLOGICAL COLLEGE

(The letter refers to the paper from the Principals of the Theological Colleges: See Appendix G)

I do not disagree with most of the document as it stands, but it seems to me substantially an argument for the maintenance of the status quo with a few modifications, and I do not think this is adequate in the current situation. The document does not take sufficiently seriously the present situation in ordained ministry in the Church and the developments which are currently occurring; and nor does it make any attempt to consider likely developments in the future. It therefore does not address with sufficient urgency the question - "what kind of training should the Church be developing to serve the whole ministry of God over the next fifteen to twenty-five years".

In particular, it seems to me that there is insufficient attention given to a number of major questions:

- to possible development in local non-stipendiary ministry in the forms of training which might be appropriate to that, and to the concepts of teamwork which local ministry will require;

- to the relation between part-time and full-time theological education, and the possibility of developing more flexible, modular patterns of training which would combine part-time and full-time elements, maintain the quality of the Church's ministry, and possibly do so at less cost than the current forms of training;

- to the independence of the Colleges, the ecclesiology underlying this independence, the difficulties of establishing a coherent training strategy for the whole Church when it has to be served by fourteen independent units, and the disadvantages of maintaining the different traditions of the Church in separate training institutions;

- to the development of an overall strategy for training which might involve the redeployment of resources away from those areas where there is at present a heavy concentration, into areas where there is now no full-time Anglican theological education at all.

I think that these questions should have been addressed more fully in the document in an open and positive way, and that they are of great importance if the Church is to develop an overall and coherent strategy for theological education which will serve the Church well into the next century. I greatly regret the fact that some of these questions (eg. questions about the independence of the Colleges) have been treated in a way which I consider seriously unsatisfactory. I accept that much of the material in the document is useful and important, but I hope that the Advisory Group will be able to give careful attention to some of the wider questions which seem to me also to be of great importance if a good overall strategy is to be worked out.

Philip Crowe
Principal

APPENDIX I

FURTHER DEGREES PANEL

Criteria to be used in assessing applications

The following criteria summarise the current policy of the Advisory Board of Ministry as endorsed by the House of Bishops.

The criteria are to be viewed in relation to one another, rather than a single criterion being considered in isolation of the full range. *The overall aim is to encourage potential theological teachers and educators.* The criteria will be reviewed in July 1992 in the light of the Panel's work.

Personal Potential and Aptitude

1. The educational criteria set for the Further Degrees Panel mean that the applicants should be of proven academic ability. This requires either an upper second or first class degree in theology or in a non-theological subject, or attainment of this standard on a degree course while in initial theological training. Applicants who *narrowly* failed to achieve a 2:1 may be considered by the panel provided written evidence from a University or CNAA College confirms their overall academic ability.

    Question: Does the candidate give evidence of this educational potential?

2. In each case, there should be the potential to gain appropriate educational skills and academic qualifications, as well as the capacity to communicate knowledge effectively and to do so in the light of the practice of the Church's ministry. Applicants must therefore demonstrate the potential to be able trainers of clergy and laity in posts such as on the staff of theological Colleges and Courses. In each case, the interviews together with the applicant's papers and the Bishops' Selectors' Report will be of assistance.

    Question: Is there evidence of teaching potential and a wish on the part of the candidate to serve in the future in such a way?

Research Proposal

3. The topic for post-graduate research (or in some cases, post-graduate study) will need to be coherent in itself. The application should include a reference from the University or CNAA College which will supervise the research. This will need to indicate the willingness in principle to accept the research proposal.

   All subjects in theology can be considered. The panel will have particular regard to research topics which are central to the concerns of the main theological subjects taught, especially those in which teachers are the most difficult to appoint. Since the research is being undertaken in response to the Church's needs, the individual student's preference for a particular topic will be considered in this wider context.

   Question: Is the topic acceptable as coherent in itself and in accord with the Church's priorities?

   Note: The panel will bear in mind the need of the Church in its education of the Church's ministers. Advice on suitable ways of approaching or understanding a proposed topic can be given by the Further Degrees Panel. Panel members can consult with each other in giving such advice.

4. It is essential that the post-graduate research is part of an overall plan for ministerial training and formation as it is not proposed that the requirements of training for ordained ministry will be waived. In cases where full-time theological research is envisaged, it will be necessary to explain how, and at what stages, the ordinand will be taking part in the life and programme of the College or Course.

   Question: Is there a satisfactory plan for ministerial training proposed by the College or Course and diocese?

5. The papers from the College or Course and diocese will need to demonstrate full support for the proposals, especially in the light of the financial implications for claims on central church funds and/or diocese for the support of both single and married ordinands.

   Question: Do the College or Course and diocese give full support?

ANNEX

Criteria for candidates aged over 30 with upper second or first class degrees who wish to read a degree in theology

Candidates with proven academic ability in these terms would, if aged under 30, qualify to read for a degree in theology.

Those in this category aged over 30 can therefore be considered for approval on educational grounds, provided that the proposal for training ensures that the wider needs of ministerial formation will be addressed. The criteria endorsed by the House of Bishops ask for an assessment of whether the person has, as a result of obtaining the degree, the potential to become at some future date, a theological teacher in theological Colleges or Courses or institutions of higher education or in schools. That a candidate has a strong personal wish to read for a degree, or is deemed academically able to do so, is not necessarily to be regarded as sufficient grounds for approval to be granted.

APPENDIX J

COUNCIL OF CHURCH & ASSOCIATED COLLEGES

Resources for Education of Clergy in the Church Colleges

INTRODUCTION

1. The object of this paper is to list some of the resources in the Church Colleges which might be deployed for the education and training of clergy.

Background: The Work of the Church Colleges

2. The Church Colleges are all independent charities. They own their sites and many of their buildings, although the DFE (Department for Education) has a reversionary interest in some of the buildings (which the former Department of Education and Science (DES) helped to finance) should they cease to be used for educational purposes.

3. In theory, the Colleges can offer educational programmes of their own choice; in practice, their freedom of action is somewhat circumscribed by the Polytechnics and Colleges Funding Council (PCFC) which funds much of their work, universities (or, decreasingly, the CNAA) which validate it, and the HMI who inspect it - the inspection reports feeding back into the PCFC's funding procedures. In line with government policy for the funding Councils, the proportion of the Colleges' income represented by PCFC grant is diminishing; the proportion represented by fees is increasing.

4. During the reorganisation of teacher training in the 1970s, several Church Colleges were closed (eg Culham, Hockerill, Sarum St Michael, St Peter's Saltley); others merged with secular institutions and effectively ceased to be Church Colleges (eg All Saints Tottenham, Bishop Lonsdale College Derby, St Luke's Exeter, St Mathias Bristol). Other Colleges joined together to form federal institutions (as at Liverpool, Roehampton and West Sussex); in Birmingham, Newman College and Westhill College operate for academic purposes as a single administrative entity.

5. Currently, (June 1992), 19 institutions with varying types of church-relatedness are in membership of the Council for Church and Associated Colleges. The 18 in England receive funds through the PCFC; Trinity College, Carmarthen receives funds through the Welsh Office. As listed in the CCAC database, and with religious affiliations in brackets, they are:

Bishop Grosseteste College, Lincoln (Anglican);

Cheltenham & Gloucester College of Higher Education (Anglican);

Chester College (Anglican);

Christ Church College of Higher Education,Canterbury (Anglican);

Homerton College, Cambridge (originally Congregational);

King Alfred's College, Winchester (Anglican);

LSU La Sainte Union College of Higher Education, Southampton (Roman Catholic);

Liverpool Institute of Higher Education (Christ's and Notre Dame: Roman Catholic + St Katherine's: Anglican);

Newman College (Roman Catholic)/Westhill College (Free Church/ecumenical), Birmingham;

College of Ripon & York St John (Anglican);

Roehampton Institute (Digby Stuart: Roman Catholic + Froebel College + Southlands: Methodist + Whitelands:Anglican);

S.Martin's College, Lancaster (Anglican);

College of St Mark & St John, Plymouth (Anglican);

St Mary's College, Twickenham (Roman Catholic);

Trinity & All Saints College, Leeds (Roman Catholic);

West London Institute of Higher Education (British & Foreign School Society);

Westminster College, Oxford (Methodist);

West Sussex Institute of Higher Education (Bishop Otter College, Chichester:Anglican + Bognor Regis College:LEA);

Trinity College, Carmarthen (Anglican).

6. The Colleges still have most of their work (47%) in teacher education. Most Colleges are, however, involved in vigorous diversification with expanding programmes of work in programme 6 (health and social services) and programme 7 (humanities and social sciences). Responding to increasing demands from adults for part-time education, Colleges are building significant portfolios of work with both PCFC funding and with funding from other sources. Some Colleges are active in teaching theology, religious education, and religious studies.

Possible areas of collaboration

a) Sharing of services of teaching staff

7. Although some of the teaching staff of the Colleges work in the area of Religious Studies (applying insights from sociology and psychology to the study of religion, sometimes without any confessional or denominational commitment), many are active in areas likely to be of interest to those responsible for either the full-time or the part-time education and training of clergy or both. Indeed, some college staff already contribute to part-time ordination courses - eg Chester, Christ Church Canterbury, and Roehampton Institute.

8. Some Theological Colleges and Courses have relatively few staff in specific subject areas so that the absence of an individual (through illness or other mishap) might severely damage a programme of teaching. They might benefit by drawing selectively on the services of individuals in a region.

9. Likewise, Colleges and Courses may wish to list appropriate Theological College staff as visiting tutors not only to add lustre to their lists but also to offer students a variety of teachers.

(b) Shared Library Facilities

10. Several Colleges and Courses already offer access to their libraries to diocesan clergy and/or part-time students on theology courses. With the cost of books and periodicals running ahead of inflation, there might be much merit in planning buying on a regional basis. The electronic data-processing being introduced to many university and college libraries makes it possible to keep detailed track of categories of user so that negotiations on shares of funding could be well-informed.

(c) Associate Membership of Common Rooms

11. Church Colleges could be invited to offer associate membership to ordinands - offering opportunities to take part in collegial activities (dinners, dramatic productions, clubs and societies, seminars and debates, talks by visiting speakers, family open-days and so forth). Such opportunities might be valued by students studying on their own in part-time courses.

12. Likewise, Theological Colleges and Courses could open their doors to neighbouring Colleges on special occasions. Joint meals of Church College and Theological College or Course staff might be the prelude to academic forms of collaboration. Both types of opportunity would require active promotion.

(d) Shared use of Residential Facilities

13. Already, some Theological Colleges have students from Church Colleges as lodgers. As most Church Colleges are currently suffering acute accommodation problems (following unexpectedly large intakes in 1991), any further offers from appropriately sited Theological Colleges will no doubt be welcomed.

14. Part-time courses for clergy might well use the facilities of Church Colleges during vacations. Most Colleges not only have good conference-standard residential accommodation, but also have

chapels, libraries, and well-equipped teaching rooms (with modern audio-visual equipment).

(e) **Shared Teaching Facilities**

15. Church Colleges are keen to have their facilities put to use for as many hours of the day and days of the year as possible. For example, facilities for instruction in information technology (for word-processing, spread-sheet analysis, data-base management, etc.) are very expensive, with frequent and substantial increases in the capabilities of personal computers (PCs) including lap-top computers. Some collaborations in the use of information technology between Church Colleges and Theological Colleges are already in place, eg in Oxford; others could be if Church Colleges were to be asked for help.

16. Church Colleges may have a growing interest in establishing outposts in towns other than those in which the Colleges are situated. The current pressure for trainee teachers to spend more time in supervised work in schools is likely to produce logistical (as well as staffing) problems for Colleges. Likewise, several Theological Colleges have established outposts for placements and may wish to increase options in collaborations with Church Colleges.

17. The Urban Learning Foundation in the East End of London is a model of good practice in this area. Founded as an initiative of the College of St Mark and St John (Marjons) when it moved from London to Plymouth, the foundation is now jointly managed by Marjons, Christ Church College Canterbury, King Alfred's College Winchester, and St Martin's College Lancaster. Some Theological Colleges already use the foundation for placements.

(f) **Shared Technical Services**

18. A fertile area for collaboration might be in the areas of finance, estates, and personnel. Most Church Colleges have, or had until recently, bursars who looked after all of these matters. Increasingly, the assumption is being made by the PCFC (and will no doubt be made by the proposed Higher Education Funding Council (HEFC)) that institutions have specialists in each of the three areas. Indeed, so complex have the legislation and related administrative processes become that some Colleges were already collaborating with other

agencies before the PCFC pressed them to do so - for example, by having payroll administration carried out by the local town hall.

19. Most Theological Colleges will no doubt wish to have someone locally (if not in the college) to call on when pipes burst, or the roof leaks, or the power fails. They may, however, wish to consider drawing on the services of Church Colleges when their present bursars retire. The consequent economies of scale in unit overheads costs would be attractive to both types of institution.

(g) Shared Insights on Models of Professional Formation

20. Church Colleges and Theological Colleges/Courses have a common interest in designing courses which interweave thought and action, theory and practice, in complex ways. As the HEFC establishes a transbinary Audit and Assessment Unit (a sort of super CNAA), Church Colleges may wish to run dress-rehearsal academic audits before they are "gone over" by the HEFC. The insights of sympathetic but critical outsiders might be welcomed for this purpose.

21. Likewise, Theological Colleges and Courses might wish to draw on the expertise of Church College staff for the regular, quinquennial review of their courses required by their validating agency, the Advisory Board of Ministry. Some college staff have served as bishops' inspectors; others might serve in a less formal, but equally formative, capacity if asked to do so.

22. Even if shared courses do not prove feasible, (and there have been some unsuccessful attempts in the past to run them), Church Colleges and Theological Colleges and Courses might find various ways of collaborating if they took part in regular, systematic, stringent yet informal course reviews.

(h) Interweaving of Professional Practices

23. There may be merit in establishing activities through which ordinands, trainee teachers, and trainee nurses (and other students) had the opportunity to meet and learn from each other. The logistics of Theological College and Course placements, nurse-education, and teacher-training are so complex that this might have to be achieved by special day-conferences. Whatever the administrative expedient

used, there should be value in permitting and encouraging students preparing for the "front-line professions" to meet regularly to explore one anothers' professional concerns.

Establishing a Framework of Collaboration

24. On 12 November 1991, there was a useful exchange of ideas between the Bishop of Lincoln, John Newton, and Brian Russell and the Chairman's Advisory Group of the CCAC. The requirement was identified for an effective two-way flow of information - to prevent, for example, administrative actions that might preempt more fruitful longer-term liaison between CCAC institutions and institutions concerned with training the clergy for any of the churches. For example, it might be inadvisable for a Church College to set up a new degree-course in theology/religious studies without detailed consultation about the disposition of scarce resources.

25. More positively, many opportunities for collaboration are starting to emerge as the education and training of the clergy come to be seen more as part of a seamless robe involving the education of all church people than as something entirely separate, even monastic. In particular, if the moment of selection for training for the ministry (especially for those under 25) could be deferred until after a period of higher education, the Church Colleges could begin to take on a significant role in the education and training of potential clergy. The ACCM working party report *Call to Order*: Vocation and Ministry in the Church of England (ACCM:1989) recognises this (vid.para.148, p.74):

"Colleges and Courses are aware that the time spent in training is also a time of testing and waiting. The loss of a student after one or two years training raises emotional and financial difficulties. Nevertheless, it is important that this training should be generally understood as part of the process of vocational exploration and community selection rather than the consequence of a selection already completed."

26. The present paper necessarily offers my personal views (although I have consulted widely in the Church Colleges and taken part in meetings of the Advisory Group on Full-Time Theological Training). I hope that it does no violence to the views of either group. However, there might be merit in establishing longer-term links between the

Church Colleges and those responsible for both full-time and part-time training for the ministry. Whether or not there is cross-representation at national level (for example between the Advisory Board of Ministry of the General Synod and the Board of Education), there will be value in regional consultation.

Sinclair Goodlad
Executive Consultant to the CCAC, Imperial College of Science,Technology, & Medicine, London SW7 2BX

11 June 1992

APPENDIX K

Theological College and Course Fees Approved by ACCM/ABM for the Five Years from 1988/89 to 1992/93

COLLEGES

	1988/89	1989/90	1990/91	1991/92	1992/93
Chichester	4,386	4,824	5,352	5,691	6,033
Cranmer Hall	4,308	4,779	5,229	5,649	5,940
Lincoln	4,155	4,710	5,385	5,832	6,087
Mirfield	2,832	2,898	3,186	3,441	3,441
Oak Hill	4,035	4,434	5,001	5,502	5,790
Queen's	4,008	4,641	4,662	5,034	5,235
Ridley Hall	4,320	4,806	5,451	5,961	6,198
Ripon, Cuddesdon	4,218	4,752	5,220	5,532	5,865
St John's, Nottm	4,191	4,455	5,091	5,499	5,775
St Stephen's House	4,047	4,719	5,199	5,601	5,880
Salisbury and Wells	4,353	4,500	4,995	5,496	5,826
Trinity	4,218	4,764	5,124	5,535	5,871
Westcott House	4,302	4,710	5,277	5,700	6,075
Wycliffe Hall	4,185	4,701	5,385	5,898	6,000
Average fee, excluding Mirfield	4,210	4,677	5,182	5,610	5,890
Percentage increase in average fee		11.09%	10.80%	8.26%	4.99%

Notes:

1. *This table sets out the College fee per student approved by ACCM/ABM for each of the five academic years to 1992/93.*

2. *The average fee is a simple average of the College fees shown in this table, excluding Mirfield which is abnormally low due to*

effective subsidies, and has not been weighted to take account of the numbers of students in each College.

COURSES

	1988/89	**1989/90**	**1990/91**	**1991/92**	**1992/93**
Canterbury	1,434	1,497	1,977	2,202	2,313
Carlisle	1,620	1,695	1,956	2,130	2,260
E. Anglia	1,800	2,010	2,115	2,298	2,436
E. Midlands - Cert.	1,506	1,605	1,734	1,842	1,995
- Dip.				1,941	2,094
Gloucester	1,260	1,941	2,076	2,244	2,355
NEOC	1,800	1,926	2,040	2,040	2,148
NOC	1,785	1,885	2,022	2,139	2,190
Oak Hill	1,504	1,683	1,899	2,052	2,154
Oxford	1,800	1,860	1,860	2,001	2,121
St Albans	1,800	1,941	2,100	2,247	2,388
SDMTS	1,557	1,650	1,812	1,989	2,106
Southwark	1,713	2,010	2,115	2,298	2,430
SWMMTC	1,470	1,599	1,647	1,656	2,079
W. Midlands	1,242	1,587	1,860	2,199	2,316
Average fee	1,592	1,777	1,944	2,085	2,226
Percentage increase in average fee		10.24%	9.40%	7.25%	6.76%

Notes: 1. *This table sets out the Course fee per student approved by ACCM/ABM for each of the five academic years to 1992/93.*

2. *The average fee is a simple average of the Course fees shown in this table and has not been weighted to take account of the numbers of students on each Course.*

APPENDIX L

Financial Results of Theological Colleges for the Three Years 1988/89, 1989/90 and 1990/91

	1988/89 £	1989/90 £	1990/91 £
Chichester	(68,747)	(42,969)	(52,013)
Cranmer Hall	(20,528)	53,806	5,685
Lincoln	(18,349)	(13,583)	(35,421)
Mirfield	-	-	-
Oak Hill	28,086	2,078	(59,675)
Queen's	(7,599)	8,206	7,377
Ridley Hall	3,517	(44,867)	(41,382)
Ripon, Cuddesdon	(7,147)	(21,208)	(50,842)
St John's, Nottm	(13,205)	(41,497)	(4,657)
St Stephen's House	(40,434)	(19,748)	(46,583)
Salisbury and Wells	(37,872)	(37,610)	(46,318)
Trinity	(21,904)	(91,671)	(1,597)
Westcott House	(6,714)	(28,405)	(19,795)
Wycliffe Hall	(7,626)	(29,099)	(11,682)
	(218,522)	(306,567)	(356,903)

Notes:

1. *The above reflects the profits or (losses) of the Colleges calculated for ABM purposes and accordingly disregards those items of income and costs not taken into account by ABM when fixing fees - see footnote to para.129 of the report.*
2. *The results shown for Cranmer Hall relate to all the students at St John's College, Durham.*
3. *Mirfield is shown as making neither a profit nor a loss for the reasons given in paragraph 133.*

APPENDIX M

Net Working Capital of Theological Colleges for the Three Years to Summer 1991

	1989	1990	1991
Chichester**	(111,966)	(105,121)	(90,414)
Cranmer Hall**	(115,506)	(61,358)	(801)
Lincoln*	(14,076)	(165,713)	(244,634)
Mirfield**	1,466,864	1,255,450	1,536,615
Oak Hill*	43,082	1,251	1,141
Queen's*	1,108,668	941,563	1,099,351
Ridley Hall*	243,036	59,603	(82,083)
Ripon, Cuddesdon*	(9,682)	(512,068)	(318,564)
St John's, Nottm**	(5,950)	(21,052)	(18,800)
St Stephen's House*	(16,709)	(67,030)	(109,399)
Salisbury and Wells*	4,550	(157,257)	(57,327)
Trinity**	158,868	(101,482)	(4,930)
Westcott House*	(24,377)	(66,705)	(16,990)
Wycliffe Hall*	(142,634)	(14,210)	197,635

Notes: *1.* *The above figures are extracted from the audited accounts of the Colleges, which are made up to varying dates in the summer of each year.*

2. *The definition of working capital is set out in para.139 of the Report.*

3. *The Colleges marked * are constituted by a trust deed and those marked ** are incorporated companies limited by guarantee.*

4. *The Cranmer Hall figures relate to St John's College, Durham as a whole.*

5. *The Oak Hill figures are audited extracts relating to the College from the accounts of the Kingham Hill Trust.*

6. *The accounts of Queen's also incorporate WMMTC and Salisbury and Wells incorporate SDMTS.*

APPENDIX N

Make up of Working Capital of Theological Colleges in the Summer of 1991

	Investments at market value	Net current assets/(liabilities)	Restricted funds	Long-term loans	Repairs provision	Working capital
Chichester	-	(39,181)	(11,166)	-	(40,067)	(90,414)
Cranmer Hall	84,025	146,229	(96,855)	(43,146)	(91,054)	(801)
Lincoln	7,095	(86,229)	-	(165,500)	-	(244,634)
Mirfield	1,151,827	409,014	(34,226)	-	-	1,536,615
Oak Hill	14,192	12,449	-	(25,500)	-	1,141
Queen's	1,319,208	(21,971)	(187,270)	-	(10,616)	1,099,351
Ridley Hall	165,476	(111,200)	(136,359)	-	-	(82,083)
Ripon, Cuddesdon	19,793	(160,756)	(2,601)	(150,000)	(25,000)	(318,564)
St John's, Nottm	26,086	671	(19,189)	(26,368)	-	(18,800)
St Stephen's House	209	(35,256)	(7,161)	(67,191)	-	(109,399)
Salisbury and Wells	43,446	42,432	(32,070)	(15,000)	(96,135)	(57,327)
Trinity	1,294	204,000	(56,163)	(132,061)	(22,000)	(4,930)
Westcott House	129,507	65,580	(167,973)	-	(44,104)	(16,990)
Wycliffe Hall	969	245,197	(48,531)	-	-	197,635

Note: *The notes to Appendix M also apply to this appendix.*

Theological Colleges: Student Numbers
1982-1991

This table summarises the number of sponsored candidates in training. An analysis of **all** students training at Theological Colleges is given on the pages that follow:

College	Sponsored Candidates in Training*									
	1982	**1983**	**1984**	**1985**	**1986**	**1987**	**1988**	**1989**	**1990**	**1991**
Chichester	40	47	47	55	51	53	40	36	37	38
Cranmer Hall	75	73	65	68	84	76	75	69	62	58
Lincoln	76	72	68	71	69	66	57	53	51	53
Mirfield	37	32	34	37	38	32	28	30	28	30
Oak Hill	63	56	50	65	80	76	68	59	60	55
Queen's	39	36	32	26	28	30	27	21	30	30
Ridley Hall	53	51	50	55	51	58	59	52	48	45
Ripon, Cuddesdon	69	71	65	63	70	73	69	65	66	73
St John's,Nottm.	108	101	88	86	105	106	98	89	82	89
St Stephen's House	54	51	46	46	53	49	42	49	50	46
Salisbury&Wells	69	75	70	78	75	69	56	59	59	51
Trinity	58	57	82	78	88	83	86	75	77	78
Westcott House	46	47	49	47	48	45	48	47	40	48
Wycliffe Hall	66	68	65	78	71	68	68	66	65	63
	---	---	---	---	---	---	---	---	---	---
	853	837	811	853	911	884	821	770	755	757

* *The figures show candidates sponsored by English Bishops and training in Theological Colleges in October of each year (in addition, a few candidates trained in Theological Colleges in Scotland and Wales.)*

Theological Colleges
STUDENT NUMBERS
1982-1991

Year	Men		Women		Total	*Ord.	Other	**Intend	Other	Other	Other	Total
(Oct)	Stip	NSM	Stip	NSM	Spon-sored		Prov-inces	Select-ion	Chur-ches		Total	
Chichester												
1982	40	0	0		40		8			1	9	49
1983	47	0	0		47						0	47
1984	46	0	1	0	47		9				9	56
1985	52	0	3	0	55		5				5	60
1986	49	1	1	0	51		4				4	55
1987	52	1	0	0	53		2				2	55
1988	37	0	3	0	40	3	2				5	45
1989	31	0	5	0	36	3	1				4	40
1990	30	2	3	2	37	3	2			1	6	43
1991	34	2	2	0	38	4	2			7	13	51
Cranmer Hall												
1982	53	0	22		75	1	1			2	4	79
1983	50	0	23		73	1	2			1	4	77
1984	48	1	16	0	65	1	3				4	69
1985	55	0	13	0	68		3	2		1	6	74
1986	68	0	16	0	84		4			3	7	91
1987	60	0	16	0	76		3				3	79
1988	55	1	19	0	75			1		2	3	78
1989	56	0	13	0	69	2			9		11	80
1990	52	2	8	0	62	1			9	1	11	73
1991	45	0	12	1	58	1	1	1	12	5	20	78

* *Students already ordained.*

** *Students intending to come forward for selection.*

Year	Men		Women		Total	*Ord.	Other	**Intend	Other	Other	Other	Total
(Oct)	Stip	NSM	Stip	NSM	Sponsored		Provinces	Selection	Churches		Total	
Lincoln												
1982	63	1	12		76		3			1	4	80
1983	60	1	11		72		3				3	75
1984	57	0	11	0	68		4				4	72
1985	57	0	14	0	71		3	1		1	5	76
1986	59	0	10	0	69		4	1		2	7	76
1987	58	0	8	0	66		2		4		6	72
1988	49	0	8	0	57		3		6		9	66
1989	45	0	8	0	53	1	1		7		9	62
1990	40	0	11	0	51				8		8	59
1991	45	0	8	0	53				9		9	62
Mirfield												
1982	37	0	0		37		4				4	41
1983	31	1	0		32		7				7	39
1984	34	0	0	0	34		5				5	39
1985	37	0	0	0	37		5				5	42
1986	37	1	0	0	38		3				3	41
1987	31	1	0	0	32		3				3	35
1988	28	0	0	0	28		2				2	30
1989	30	0	0	0	30	1	2				3	33
1990	27	1	0	0	28						0	28
1991	30	0	0	0	30						0	30

Year (Oct)	Men Stip	Men NSM	Women Stip	Women NSM	Total Sponsored	*Ord.	Other Provinces	**Intend Selection	Other Churches	Other	Other Total	Total
Oak Hill												
1982	53	4	6		63	5	4			7	16	79
1983	50	1	5		56	6	1	1		8	16	72
1984	43	1	5	1	50	3		1		18	22	72
1985	53	0	10	2	65	2	2	6		18	28	93
1986	70	0	9	1	80	2	2	5		23	32	112
1987	69	0	6	1	76	2	4	3	4	14	27	103
1988	60	0	6	2	68	1	1	1	1	21	25	93
1989	52	0	7	0	59	6		3	1	19	29	88
1990	50	2	8	0	60	6				31	37	97
1991	46	1	7	1	55	4		5	1	37	47	102
Queen's												
1982	36	0	3		39	1	2			33	36	75
1983	32	0	4		36		3			31	34	70
1984	29	0	3	0	32		4			32	36	68
1985	22	1	3	0	26	6	4	1		33	44	70
1986	24	1	3	0	28	1	8			38	47	75
1987	26	0	4	0	30	1	5		42		48	78
1988	20	0	7		27				42	2	44	71
1989	16	0	5	0	21		2		47	3	52	73
1990	20	0	10	0	30		3		54	3	60	90
1991	20	0	9	1	30	3	1	1	50		55	85

Year (Oct)	Men Stip	Men NSM	Women Stip	Women NSM	Total Spon-sored	*Ord.	Other Prov-inces	**Intend Select-ion	Other Chur-ches	Other	Other Total	Total
Ridley Hall												
1982	51	1	1		53	2				1	3	56
1983	49	0	2		51	2	2				4	55
1984	47	0	3	0	50	2	2	2			6	56
1985	48	0	7	0	55	5	5	1		1	12	67
1986	46	0	5	0	51	1	5	1			7	58
1987	49	1	8	0	58	1	2		1	2	6	64
1988	47	0	11	1	59	2	1		1	3	7	66
1989	41	0	11	0	52		3		1		4	56
1990	39	0	9	0	48	2	1	1		1	5	53
1991	41	0	4	0	45		3	2		1	6	51
Ripon, Cuddesdon												
1982	62	1	6		69		3				3	72
1983	60	0	11		71	1	2				3	74
1984	53	2	10	0	65		2				2	67
1985	52	0	9	2	63	2	2			1	5	68
1986	54	2	14	0	70						0	70
1987	54	0	18	1	73		1	1			2	75
1988	47	1	20	1	69	1	2				3	72
1989	48	1	16	0	65		4			1	5	70
1990	50	0	16	0	66		2				2	68
1991	58	0	15	0	73		3				3	76

Year	Men		Women		Total	*Ord.	Other	**Intend	Other	Other	Other	Total
(Oct)	Stip	NSM	Stip	NSM	Spon-sored		Prov-inces	Select-ion	Chur-ches		Total	
St John's, Nottingham												
1982	96	0	12		108	2	6	1		15	24	132
1983	90	0	11		101	4	6			16	26	127
1984	77	2	9	0	88	5	4	6		17	32	120
1985	70	2	14	0	86	5	9	6		18	38	124
1986	92	0	13	0	105	1	7	1		14	23	128
1987	96	0	10	0	106	1	6	1	4	11	23	129
1988	82	0	15	1	98	3	5	5		9	22	120
1989	75	0	14	0	89	1	3	1	2	18	25	114
1990	72	1	9	0	82	2	4	1	1	23	31	113
1991	78	2	9	0	89	3	5	1	1	22	32	121
St Stephen's House												
1982	47	1	6		54	1	3				4	58
1983	44	0	7		51		5			2	7	58
1984	44	0	2	0	46	1	5			1	7	53
1985	42	0	4	0	46	2	7			2	11	57
1986	47	1	5	0	53		5			1	6	59
1987	43	1	5		49	1	4		1		6	55
1988	38	1	3	0	42		5			1	6	48
1989	43	2	4	0	49	4	4			1	9	58
1990	47	0	3	0	50		7		1	3	11	61
1991	41	0	5	0	46	1	4	3		1	9	55

Year	Men		Women		Total	*Ord.	Other	**Intend	Other	Other	Other	Total
(Oct)	Stip	NSM	Stip	NSM	Sponsored		Provinces	Selection	Churches		Total	
Salisbury & Wells												
1982	66	1	2		69	1	6				7	76
1983	70	1	4		75	2	5				7	82
1984	65	0	5	0	70	2	5	2			9	79
1985	70	0	8	0	78	1	3				4	82
1986	68	0	7	0	75		5			1	6	81
1987	62	0	7	0	69	1	5			1	7	76
1988	49	1	6	0	56	2	5			1	8	64
1989	44	1	13	1	59	2	3	1		1	7	66
1990	45	0	12	2	59		2				2	61
1991	44	0	7	0	51	2	4			1	7	58
Trinity												
1982	48	0	10		58	8	3	17		7	35	93
1983	46	0	11		57	12	8	3		23	46	103
1984	66	0	15	1	82	9	2	1		35	47	129
1985	61	1	15	1	78	6	3	2		44	55	133
1986	67	1	19	1	88	2		2		42	46	134
1987	62	1	19	1	83	4			8	37	49	132
1988	61	2	22	1	86	6	1			44	51	137
1989	57	0	18	0	75	9	1			34	44	119
1990	66	0	11	0	77	9	1	2		42	54	131
1991	65	0	13	0	78	11	1	4	11	62	89	167

Year	Men		Women		Total	*Ord.	Other	**Intend	Other	Other	Other	Total
(Oct)	Stip	NSM	Stip	NSM	Spon-sored		Prov-inces	Select-ion	Chur-ches		Total	
Westcott House												
1982	39	0	7		46	1	2			1	4	50
1983	40	0	7		47	1	1			2	4	51
1984	38	1	10	0	49	1	1			1	3	52
1985	37	1	8	1	47	1	3			2	6	53
1986	36	2	10	0	48	1	2			3	6	54
1987	33	0	12	0	45	1	4			2	7	52
1988	32	0	14	2	48	1	5				6	54
1989	36	2	7	2	47	1	4			5	10	57
1990	31	0	8	1	40		4	2	1	2	9	49
1991	36	0	11	1	48	2	3	1	3		9	57
Wycliffe Hall												
1982	59	2	5		66	9	10	3		2	24	90
1983	61	1	6		68	4	12	2		2	20	88
1984	55	0	9	1	65	2	11			3	16	81
1985	66	1	7	4	78	3	5	1		2	11	89
1986	62	1	7	1	71	6	6	1		2	15	86
1987	59	0	9	0	68	3	4	3	2	7	19	87
1988	57	0	10	1	68	2	2	1	1	6	12	80
1989	56	0	9	1	66	1	3	1	2	4	11	77
1990	55	0	10	0	65	1	2			15	18	83
1991	53	0	10	0	63	2	4		7	7	20	83

Year	Men		Women		Total	*Ord.	Other	**Intend	Other	Other	Other	Total
(Oct)	Stip	NSM	Stip	NSM	Sponsored		Provinces	Selection	Churches		Total	
TOTALS												
1982	750	11	92	0	853	31	55	21	0	70	177	1030
1983	730	5	102	0	837	33	57	6	0	85	181	1018
1984	702	7	99	3	811	26	57	12	0	107	202	1013
1985	722	6	115	10	853	33	59	20	0	123	235	1088
1986	779	10	119	3	911	14	55	11	0	129	209	1120
1987	754	5	122	3	884	15	45	8	66	74	208	1092
1988	662	6	144	9	821	21	34	8	51	89	203	1024
1989	630	6	130	4	770	31	31	6	69	86	223	993
1990	624	8	118	5	755	24	28	6	74	122	254	1009
1991	636	5	112	4	757	33	31	18	94	143	319	1076

* *Students already ordained.*
** *Students intending to come forward for selection.*

APPENDIX P

STUDENT NUMBERS FOR THE METHODIST AND UNITED REFORMED CHURCHES

1982-1991

(Neither Church keeps separate statistics for men and women)

A: SUMMARY CHART OF STUDENT MINISTERS, METHODIST CHURCH

Year	College	Courses	*CCIP	In-service	Distance	TOTAL	**Including MLA intake each year
1982/83	139	13	4			156	
1983/84	125	15	5			145	
1984/85	130	15	4			149	
1985/86	125	10	3	5		143	
1986/87	148	10	3	4		165	
1987/88	170	10	3	8		191	
1988/89	171	14	3	10		198	(12)
1989/90	172	19	2	15	3	211	(21)
1990/91	172	40	2	12	4	230	(18)
1991/92	180	56	3	11	4(+5 specials)	259	(17)

* *A combined Circuit and College Training Programme.*

** *MLA - Ministry in Local Appointment, for which Methodist candidating and training procedures are identical with those for itinerant ministry.*

Notes:

1. *From 1988/89 onwards, the figures included a number of Ministers in Local Appointment. Nevertheless the trend in numbers for itinerant circuit ministry has still been upwards.*
2. *The average age of students has risen.*
3. *Over the next two years, numbers are expected to decline a little and then level out.*

B: SUMMARY CHART OF ORDINANDS FOR MINISTRY IN THE URC

	Stipendiary Ministry	Non-Stipendiary Ministry	TOTAL
1982/83	80	80	160
1983/84	73	81	154
1984/85	78	63	141
1985/86	77	69	146
1986/87	82	72	154
1987/88	100	70	170
1988/89	112	67	179
1989/90	113	71	184
1990/91	101	78	179
1991/92	94	80	174

Notes:

1. *In the main, stipendiary candidates study in Colleges and NSM's on Courses. All stipendiaries are required to spend at least one year of full-time study on a College-directed programme. The final year is normally an Internship year, spent partly in a local church and partly in College.*
2. *Most stipendiaries spend an average 3 years full-time in College. The course may vary from one year to four, according to age, previous study and experience.*
3. *A number of stipendiaries (currently about 10%) undertake the URC Alternative Programme of 3 years' part-time study on a Course and one year in a College, including a local church placement.*
4. *Intake of stipendiary candidates peaked in 1990 and has subsequently fallen.*

APPENDIX Q

Initial Training for Ordained Ministry
A Possible Way Forward
(paper presented to the Advisory Group
by the Revd Canon Dr Joy Tetley)

OVERALL CONCEPT

1.1 Initial training would comprise a carefully constructed combination of "on the job" learning in a designated training parish (DTP), "block study" at a regional theological centre (RTC) and some element of "distance learning". The period covered would be five years, with ordination to the diaconate after two years.

1.2 Before outlining the methodology, the roles of the RTC and DTP are set out.

REGIONAL THEOLOGICAL CENTRES (SAY 5 OR 6)

2.1 The primary role of RTC's would be to provide a locus and resources for the pursuit of theological study and exploration. They would encourage and facilitate the doing of theology as thoroughly and creatively as possible within the context of the faith community but also having close working links with universities.

2.2 They would be staffed by specialist theologians, a fair proportion of whom will have had significant ministerial experience. Staffing would be on a "non party" and ecumenical basis, the major criterion being the capacity to undertake and teach Christian theology (at a whole range of levels).

2.3 RTC's would not only play a vital part in initial ordination training. They would also function as an invaluable resource for the wider Church - for example, in such areas as continuing ministerial education, preparation and in-service training for authorised lay ministries, the faith-development of the people of God.

DESIGNATED TRAINING PARISHES

3.1 At the outset of training, the ordinand (and family, where applicable) would be placed in a designated training parish. This would be the ordinand's parish and home for the whole period of initial training, though he or she would also experience a range of other placements.

3.2 Such a system would mean that the choice of "curacy parish" has to be made at the beginning of training rather than at ordination. It would also require selection of a parish on the basis of its suitability to encourage and evaluate ministerial formation. That suitability depends on a wide variety of factors, not least the willingness of the congregation to be positively involved in the enterprise of training. In effect, the diocese and parish would enter into a training contract with the ordinand. This might encourage all parties to take the matter of training (and its setting) more seriously.

3.3 The parish base would be located in the sponsoring diocese or elsewhere (as is now the case at ordination). There would clearly need to be careful consultation between the parties concerned. It may well be, for example, that an ordinand would prefer to be involved with an RTC far removed from his or her sponsoring diocese. The question of "release" would then have to be negotiated.

3.4 Under this scheme there would be even greater incentive than at present for diocesan authorities to look carefully at resources and to plan ahead, giving conscious priority to the specific needs of initial ministerial formation. In the placing of ordinands, the assurance of adequate training support would rank above both a parish's perceived need for ordained ministers and its financial resources.

3.5 The scheme would also underline the need for co-operation between dioceses. Given diocesan co-operation and continuing evaluation of a DTP, there might be less risk of curates ending up in situations which offer no proper training.

3.6 It is likely that, in a fair number of cases, the incumbent of the training parish would not be in situ for the whole five-year period (that is indeed the case for many a curate working under the present three year system!) This would not be a major obstacle if the parish church as a whole is taking a full part in the training task and if the ordinand has been assigned a local mentor/tutor to whom regular reference can be made. A change of incumbent might in fact be helpful in bringing a different perspective (cf changes of staff at theological colleges).

INGREDIENTS IN THE LEARNING PROCESS

Learning on the job by means of on-going supervised experience in the parish base.

4.1 As well as the incumbent and others in the parish, the ordinand and curate would also have a local mentor/tutor with whom to reflect on and respond to the practical experience of ministry.

4.2 Throughout the period of training there would also be provision for a variety of other short term placements in the locality.

Study Based at the RTC

4.3 Such study might be in concentrated "blocks" (several weeks at a time) on a residential or non-residential basis (depending on the distances involved).

4.4 The aim of these study periods would be to explore the theological heritage of the Christian Church and to encourage dynamic interaction between this heritage and contemporary experience, not least of the ordinand concerned. Time at the RTC would provide opportunity to hear from specialists, read, write and work with others.

4.5 The first study block should be early on in the training period, after allowing a short time (say a month) to settle in the parish base and begin to establish routine and relationships.

Distance Learning

4.6 This would be organised by the RTC in co-operation with the training parish to enable the ordinand to continue structural and assessed theological study in the context of the parish base.

Qualification

4.7 Most would work for a university validated degree in theology and ministerial studies, a degree which would take into account the candidate's total learning experience.

4.8 There would, however, be enough flexibility in the scheme for people, as appropriate, to pursue other avenues of qualification, eg research degrees on the one hand and diplomas or certificates on the other.

FINANCE

5.1 In general, there would be something of a shift in funding from central to local. (Any significant shift could be corrected by an adjustment of diocesan contributions to central funds). Maintenance would no longer be paid through the colleges, as the ordinand/curate would be receiving income and expenses in his or her parish setting. Clearly there would need to be discussion as to the appropriate level of support given in the first two years. In principle, as this is all part of the training process, it is envisaged that a stipend be paid (cf the position of student nurses, accountancy trainees).

5.2 The parish-based ministerial training would be financed on the same basis as for existing curacy placements. This varies between diocese and parishes. For a parish used to catering for curates, this would present no additional financial burden (they would simply be paying for *one* "curate" over five years, rather than two in succession). There would no doubt have to be a change in attitudes. As a key constituent in the training process, they would need to release their "learner" for far more significant periods than has hitherto been required by POT. Furthermore, if the concept of DTP's is taken seriously, some parishes at present enjoying curates might no longer qualify. There might then be consequent changes in funding within a diocese.

5.2 Fees and expenses incurred through study at the RTC and "distance learning" would be covered by a grant system from central church funds.

5.3 There would be no need for the diocese (or TAP) to make specific provision for families as this would be covered by financial arrangements made in relation to the parish base.

5.4 The establishment and continuing financial viability of the RTC's would be considerably helped if existing theological colleges were persuaded of the need to pool their resources for the good of the whole church.

ADVANTAGES

6.1 Ordination training would become much more rigorous, thorough and creative.

6.2 The proposed system would encourage a more integrated approach to learning, theology and ministry.

6.3 There would be greater opportunity for theological teachers to pursue research and writing projects. There would be greater opportunity for theologically qualified ordinands to take their theology further.

6.4 The RTC's could become an invaluable resource for the wider Church on an ecumenical as well as Anglican basis.

6.5 Ministerial formation could become a more truly co-operative enterprise, involving diocese and parishes in a more thorough-going and detailed way than at present.

6.6 Ordinands and their families would have the security and support of a Church community for the whole of the five-year period. This might be especially important for families. It would also drastically lessen the "transition trauma" arising from the contrast between the necessarily artificial atmosphere of College and the reality of ministerial parish life - not to mention the upheaval of moving twice, with all that that involves.

6.7 There would be plenty of scope for flexibility and diversity.

6.8 Present non-residential courses could be integrated more effectively into this scheme - as could those training for non-stipendiary ministry.

6.9 Through the RTC's, theological training for ministry could become more wholeheartedly ecumenical.

CHALLENGES

7.1 The changing of attitudes and entrench positions.

7.2 The funding of the RTC's.

7.3 Redundancies in colleges. Against this, the redeployment of some gifted teachers in parishes might help support for the scheme at parish and diocesan level.

7.4 Possible difficulties in realising the value of college properties no longer required.

7.5 Obtaining adequate information to assess the financial consequences.

ENGLAND AND WALES

0 10 20 30 40 50miles

0 20 40 60 80km

Boundary between the Provinces of Canterbury and York, and between the Province of Canterbury and Wales (Church in Wales)

Diocesan boundary

County boundary

Cathedral City

The Channel Islands are annexed to the Diocese of Winchester

The Isles of Scilly are included in the Diocese of Truro

This map has been reproduced by kind permission of the Church Commissioners and the Central Board of Finance of the Church of England.

The Lancaster-Bridlington boundary (referred to in paragraph 64 of this Report) has been added.